Tkinter GUI Application Development Cookbook

A practical solution to your GUI development problems with Python and Tkinter

Alejandro Rodas de Paz

BIRMINGHAM - MUMBAI

Tkinter GUI Application Development Cookbook

Commissioning Editor: Amarabha Banerjee
Acquisition Editor: Reshma Raman
Content Development Editor: Jason Pereira
Technical Editor: Prajakta Mhatre
Copy Editor: Dhanya Baburaj
Project Coordinator: Sheejal Shah
Proofreader: Safis Editing
Indexer: Rekha Nair
Production Coordinator: Deepika Naik

First published: March 2018
Production reference: 1270318

Published by Packt Publishing Ltd.
Livery Place
35 Livery Street
Birmingham
B3 2PB, UK.

ISBN 978-1-78862-230-1

www.packtpub.com

I dedicate my work to my aunt, Elena, and my cousins, Julia and Laura. This book would not have been possible without their love and support.

`mapt.io`

Mapt is an online digital library that gives you full access to over 5,000 books and videos, as well as industry leading tools to help you plan your personal development and advance your career. For more information, please visit our website.

Why subscribe?

- Spend less time learning and more time coding with practical eBooks and Videos from over 4,000 industry professionals

- Improve your learning with Skill Plans built especially for you

- Get a free eBook or video every month

- Mapt is fully searchable

- Copy and paste, print, and bookmark content

PacktPub.com

Did you know that Packt offers eBook versions of every book published, with PDF and ePub files available? You can upgrade to the eBook version at `www.PacktPub.com` and as a print book customer, you are entitled to a discount on the eBook copy. Get in touch with us at `service@packtpub.com` for more details.

At `www.PacktPub.com`, you can also read a collection of free technical articles, sign up for a range of free newsletters, and receive exclusive discounts and offers on Packt books and eBooks.

Contributors

About the author

Alejandro Rodas de Paz is a computer engineer from Seville, Spain. He has developed several projects with Python, from web crawlers to artificial intelligence algorithms. He has also used Tkinter for building an application for the lighting system of the city of Almere (Netherlands).

Prior to this publication, Alejandro co-wrote Packt's title *Python Game Development by Example*, and collaborated as a technical reviewer on the book *Tkinter GUI Application Development Hotshot*.

I would like to thank the exceptional team at Packt Publishing for their assistance during this journey, and words cannot express my gratitude to Jason and Prajakta for their understanding and immense patience.

About the reviewers

Javier Becerra Elcinto received his PhD in image processing from the Université de Bordeaux in 2006. In 2010 he started working as a self-employed developer working with Python and C++, and in 2014 he cofounded Panoimagen S.L. There, he has continued to develop software for industrial and precision agriculture applications. Javier lectures regularly on scientific programming in private companies and several Spanish research institutions.

Marcos Perez Gonzalez works in the treatment of multimedia document databases with Python. Previously, he had been using it as glue between projects and technologies for more than 10 years. At the beginning of his career, he used Python for embedding purposes and multiplatform GUI programming.

He is a member of the Python Spain association and the Python Madrid meetup. Moreover, he has been a member of the board of directors of the Spanish Association of Computer Engineering.

He holds a master's degree in computer engineering from the University of Valladolid.

Bryson Tyrrell is a systems development engineer at Jamf in Minneapolis, Minnesota. In addition to the responsibilities of his role, Bryson has spoken at various IT conferences (including the Jamf Nation User Conference, Penn State MacAdmins, Mac Admins and Developers UK, and Atlassian Summit) and maintains a number of open source tools for the Mac admin community on his GitHub account.

Packt is searching for authors like you

If you're interested in becoming an author for Packt, please visit `authors.packtpub.com` and apply today. We have worked with thousands of developers and tech professionals, just like you, to help them share their insight with the global tech community. You can make a general application, apply for a specific hot topic that we are recruiting an author for, or submit your own idea.

Table of Contents

Preface

As one of the more versatile programming languages, Python is well known for its batteries-included philosophy, which includes a rich set of modules in its standard library; Tkinter is the library used to build desktop applications. Built over the Tk GUI toolkit, Tkinter is a common choice for rapid GUI development, and complex applications can benefit from the full capabilities of this library. This book covers all of your Tkinter and Python GUI development problems and solutions.

Tkinter GUI Application Development Cookbook starts with an overview of Tkinter classes and at the same time provides recipes for basic topics, such as layout patterns and event handling. Next, this book covers how to develop common GUI patterns, such as entering and saving data, navigating through menus and dialogs, and performing long-running actions in the background. You can then make your apps leverage network resources effectively and perform graphical operations on a canvas and related tasks such as detecting collisions between items. Finally, this book covers using themed widgets, an extension of Tk widgets that have a more native look and feel.

By the end of the book, you will have an in-depth knowledge of Tkinter classes and know how to use them to build efficient and rich GUI applications.

Who this book is for

This book targets Python developers who are familiar with the basics of the language—syntax, data structures, and OOP—wants to learn effective solutions to the common challenges of GUI development, and desires to discover interesting capabilities that Tkinter can offer to build complex applications.

You do not need previous experience with Tkinter or other GUI development libraries since the first part of the book will teach the basics of the library through the introductory use cases.

What this book covers

Chapter 1, *Getting Started with Tkinter*, introduces the structure of a Tkinter program and shows you how to perform the most common tasks, such as creating widgets and handling user events.

Chapter 2, *Window Layout*, demonstrates how to place widgets using geometry managers and improve the layout of large applications.

Chapter 3, *Customizing Widgets*, dives deeper into Tkinter's widget configuration and appearance customization.

Chapter 4, *Dialogs and Menus*, teaches you how to improve the navigation of Tkinter apps with menus and dialogs.

Chapter 5, *Object-Oriented Programming and MVC*, teaches you how to effectively apply design patterns in your Tkinter applications.

Chapter 6, *Asynchronous Programming*, covers several recipes to execute long-running actions without freezing the application—a recurring problem in GUI development.

Chapter 7, *Canvas and Graphics*, explores the Canvas widget and the types of items you can add to the canvas and how to manipulate them.

Chapter 8, *Themed Widgets*, teaches you how to extend Tkinter applications with the Tk-themed widget set.

To get the most out of this book

To get up and running, users will need to have the following technologies installed:

- Python 3.x
- Any operating system

Download the example code files

You can download the example code files for this book from your account at www.packtpub.com. If you purchased this book elsewhere, you can visit www.packtpub.com/support and register to have the files emailed directly to you.

You can download the code files by following these steps:

1. Log in or register at `www.packtpub.com`.
2. Select the **SUPPORT** tab.
3. Click on **Code Downloads & Errata**.
4. Enter the name of the book in the **Search** box and follow the onscreen instructions.

Once the file is downloaded, please make sure that you unzip or extract the folder using the latest version of:

- WinRAR/7-Zip for Windows
- Zipeg/iZip/UnRarX for Mac
- 7-Zip/PeaZip for Linux

The code bundle for the book is also hosted on GitHub at `https://github.com/PacktPublishing/Tkinter-GUI-Application-Development-Cookbook`. In case there's an update to the code, it will be updated on the existing GitHub repository.

We also have other code bundles from our rich catalog of books and videos available at `https://github.com/PacktPublishing/`. Check them out!

Download the color images

We also provide a PDF file that has color images of the screenshots/diagrams used in this book. You can download it here: `https://www.packtpub.com/sites/default/files/downloads/TkinterGUIApplicationDevelopmentCookbook_ColorImages.pdf`.

Conventions used

There are a number of text conventions used throughout this book.

`CodeInText`: Indicates code words in text, database table names, folder names, filenames, file extensions, pathnames, dummy URLs, user input, and Twitter handles. Here is an example: "The `delete()` method takes two arguments that indicate the range of the characters that should be deleted."

A block of code is set as follows:

```
from tkinter import *

root = Tk()
btn = Button(root, text="Click me!")
btn.config(command=lambda: print("Hello, Tkinter!"))
btn.pack(padx=120, pady=30)
root.title("My Tkinter app")
root.mainloop()
```

When we wish to draw your attention to a particular part of a code block, the relevant lines or items are set in bold:

```
def show_caption(self, event):
    caption = tk.Label(self, ...)
    caption.place(in_=event.widget, x=event.x, y=event.y)
    # ...
```

Bold: Indicates a new term, an important word, or words that you see onscreen. For example, words in menus or dialog boxes appear in the text like this. Here is an example: "The first will be labeled **Choose file**."

Warnings or important notes appear like this.

Tips and tricks appear like this.

Get in touch

Feedback from our readers is always welcome.

General feedback: Email feedback@packtpub.com and mention the book title in the subject of your message. If you have questions about any aspect of this book, please email us at questions@packtpub.com.

Errata: Although we have taken every care to ensure the accuracy of our content, mistakes do happen. If you have found a mistake in this book, we would be grateful if you would report this to us. Please visit www.packtpub.com/submit-errata, selecting your book, clicking on the Errata Submission Form link, and entering the details.

Piracy: If you come across any illegal copies of our works in any form on the Internet, we would be grateful if you would provide us with the location address or website name. Please contact us at copyright@packtpub.com with a link to the material.

If you are interested in becoming an author: If there is a topic that you have expertise in and you are interested in either writing or contributing to a book, please visit authors.packtpub.com.

Reviews

Please leave a review. Once you have read and used this book, why not leave a review on the site that you purchased it from? Potential readers can then see and use your unbiased opinion to make purchase decisions, we at Packt can understand what you think about our products, and our authors can see your feedback on their book. Thank you!

For more information about Packt, please visit packtpub.com.

1
Getting Started with Tkinter

In this chapter, we will cover the following recipes:

- Structuring a Tkinter application
- Working with buttons
- Creating text entries
- Tracing text changes
- Validating a text entry
- Selecting numerical values
- Creating selections with radio buttons
- Implementing switches with checkboxes
- Displaying a list of items
- Handling mouse and keyboard events
- Setting the main window's icon, title, and size

Introduction

Thanks to its clear syntax and the wide ecosystem of libraries and tools, Python has become a popular and general-purpose programming language. From web development to **Natural Language Processing (NLP)**, you can easily find an open source library that fits the need of your application domain, and in the last instance, you can always use any of the modules included in the Python standard library.

The standard library follows the "batteries-included" philosophy, which means that it contains a large collection of utilities: regular expressions, mathematical functions, networking, and so on. The standard **Graphical User Interface (GUI)** package of this library is **Tkinter**, a thin object-oriented layer on top of Tcl/Tk.

Starting from Python 3, the `Tkinter` module was renamed to `tkinter` (with a lowercase **t**). It also affects to the `tkinter.ttk` and `tkinter.tix` extensions. We will dive into the `tkinter.ttk` module in the last chapter of this book, since the `tkinter.tix` module is officially deprecated.

In this chapter, we will explore several patterns for some basic classes of the `tkinter` module and some methods that are common to all widget subclasses.

Structuring a Tkinter application

One of the main advantages of making applications with Tkinter is that it is very easy to set up a basic GUI with a script of a few lines. As the programs get more complex, it becomes more difficult to separate logically each part, so an organized structure will help us to keep our code clean.

Getting ready

We will take the following program as an example:

```
from tkinter import *

root = Tk()
btn = Button(root, text="Click me!")
btn.config(command=lambda: print("Hello, Tkinter!"))
btn.pack(padx=120, pady=30)
root.title("My Tkinter app")
root.mainloop()
```

It creates a main window with a button that prints `Hello, Tkinter!` in the console each time it is clicked. The button is placed with a padding of 120px in the horizontal axis and 30px in the vertical axis. The last statement starts the main loop, which processes user events and updates the GUI until the main window is destroyed:

```
Python 3.6.4 (v3.6.4:d48eceb, Dec 19 2017, 06:04:45) [MSC v.1900 32 bit (Intel)] on win32
Type "help", "copyright", "credits" or "license" for more information.
>>> from tkinter import *
>>> root = Tk()
>>> btn = Button(root, text= "Click me!")
>>> btn.config(command=lambda: print("Hello, Tkinter!"))
>>> btn.pack(padx=120, pady=30)
>>> root.title("My Tkinter app")

>>> root.mainloop()
Hello, Tkinter!
Hello, Tkinter!
```

You can execute the program and verify that it is working as expected. However, all our variables are defined in the global namespace, and the more widgets you add, the more difficult it becomes to reason about the parts where they are used.

Wildcard imports (`from ... import *`) are strongly discouraged in production code because they pollute your global namespace—we only used them here to illustrate an anti-pattern that can be commonly seen in online examples.

These maintainability issues can be addressed with basic OOP techniques, which are considered good practice in all types of Python programs.

How to do it...

To improve the modularity of our simple program, we will define a class that wraps our global variables:

```python
import tkinter as tk

class App(tk.Tk):
    def __init__(self):
        super().__init__()
        self.btn = tk.Button(self, text="Click me!",
                             command=self.say_hello)
        self.btn.pack(padx=120, pady=30)

    def say_hello(self):
        print("Hello, Tkinter!")

if __name__ == "__main__":
    app = App()
    app.title("My Tkinter app")
    app.mainloop()
```

Now, each variable is enclosed in a specific scope, including the command function, which is moved as a separate method.

How it works...

First, we replaced the wildcard import with the import ... as syntax to have better control over our global namespace.

Then, we defined our App class as a Tk subclass, which now is referenced via the tk namespace. To properly initialize the base class, we will call the __init__ method of the Tk class with the built-in super() function. This corresponds to the following lines:

```
class App(tk.Tk):
    def __init__(self):
        super().__init__()
        # ...
```

Now, we have a reference to the App instance with the self variable, so we will add all the Button widget as an attribute of our class.

Although it may look overkill for such a simple program, this refactoring will help us to reason about each part, the button instantiation is separated from the callback that gets executed when it is clicked, and the application bootstrapping is moved to the if __name__ == "__main__" block, which is a common practice in executable Python scripts.

We will follow this convention through all the code samples, so you can take this template as the starting point of any larger application.

There's more...

We subclassed the Tk class in our example, but it is also common to subclass other widget classes. We did this to reproduce the same statements that we had before we refactored the code.

However, it may be more convenient to subclass Frame or Toplevel in larger programs, such as those with multiple windows. This is because a Tkinter application should have only one Tk instance, and the system creates one automatically if you instantiate a widget before you create the Tk instance.

Keep in mind that this decision does not affect the structure of our App class since all widget classes have a `mainloop` method that internally starts the Tk main loop.

Working with buttons

Button widgets represent a clickable item of your GUI applications. They typically use a text or an image indicating the action that will be performed when clicked. Tkinter allows you to easily configure this functionality with some standard options of the Button widget class.

How to do it...

The following contains a button with an image that gets disabled when clicked and a list of buttons with the different types of available reliefs:

```python
import tkinter as tk

RELIEFS = [tk.SUNKEN, tk.RAISED, tk.GROOVE, tk.RIDGE, tk.FLAT]

class ButtonsApp(tk.Tk):
    def __init__(self):
        super().__init__()
        self.img = tk.PhotoImage(file="python.gif")
        self.btn = tk.Button(self, text="Button with image",
                             image=self.img, compound=tk.LEFT,
                             command=self.disable_btn)
        self.btns = [self.create_btn(r) for r in RELIEFS]
        self.btn.pack()
        for btn in self.btns:
            btn.pack(padx=10, pady=10, side=tk.LEFT)

    def create_btn(self, relief):
        return tk.Button(self, text=relief, relief=relief)

    def disable_btn(self):
        self.btn.config(state=tk.DISABLED)

if __name__ == "__main__":
    app = ButtonsApp()
    app.mainloop()
```

The purpose of this program is to show several configuration options that can be used when creating a Button widget.

After executing the preceding code, you will get the following output:

How it works...

The most basic way of instantiation of `Button` is using the `text` option to set the button label and the command option that references the function to be invoked when the button is clicked.

In out example, we also added `PhotoImage` via the `image` option, which takes precedence over the *text* string. The `compound` option serves to combine image and text in the same button, determining the position where the image is placed. It accepts the following constants as valid values: `CENTER`, `BOTTOM`, `LEFT`, `RIGHT`, and `TOP`.

The second row of buttons is created with a list comprehension, using the list of `RELIEF` values. The label of each button corresponds to the name of the constant, so you can note the difference in the appearance of each button.

There's more...

We used an attribute to keep a reference to our `PhotoImage` instance, even though we are not using it outside our __init__ method. The reason is that images are cleared when they are garbage collected, which will happen if we declare it as a local variable and the method exists.

To avoid this, always remember to keep a reference to each `PhotoImage` object as long as the window where it is shown is still alive.

Creating text entries

The Entry widget represents a text input displayed in a single line. Along with the `Label` and `Button` classes, it is one of the most commonly used Tkinter classes.

How to do it...

This example shows how to create a login form with two entry instances for the `username` and `password` fields. Each character of `password` is displayed as an asterisk to avoid showing it in clear text:

```python
import tkinter as tk

class LoginApp(tk.Tk):
    def __init__(self):
        super().__init__()
        self.username = tk.Entry(self)
        self.password = tk.Entry(self, show="*")
        self.login_btn = tk.Button(self, text="Log in",
                                   command=self.print_login)
        self.clear_btn = tk.Button(self, text="Clear",
                                   command=self.clear_form)
        self.username.pack()
        self.password.pack()
        self.login_btn.pack(fill=tk.BOTH)
        self.clear_btn.pack(fill=tk.BOTH)

    def print_login(self):
        print("Username: {}".format(self.username.get()))
        print("Password: {}".format(self.password.get()))

    def clear_form(self):
        self.username.delete(0, tk.END)
        self.password.delete(0, tk.END)
        self.username.focus_set()

if __name__ == "__main__":
    app = LoginApp()
    app.mainloop()
```

The `Log in` button prints the values in the console, whereas the `Clear` button removes the content of both entries and returns the focus to the entry for `username`:

How it works...

The Entry widgets are instantiated using the parent window or frame as the first argument and a set of optional keyword arguments to configure additional options. We did not specify any options for the entry corresponding to the `username` field. To keep the password secret, we specify the `show` argument with the string `"*"`, which will display each typed character as an asterisk.

With the `get()` method, we will retrieve the current text as a string. This is used in the `print_login` method to show the entries' content in the standard output.

The `delete()` method takes two arguments that indicate the range of the characters that should be deleted. Keep in mind that the indices start at the position 0, and they do not include the character at the end of the range. If only one argument is passed, it deletes the character at that position.

In the `clear_form()` method, we delete from index 0 to the constant END, which means that the whole content is removed. Finally, we set the focus to the `username` entry.

There's more...

The content of an Entry widget can be modified programmatically with the `insert()` method, which takes two arguments:

- `index`: The position to insert the text; note that entry positions are 0-indexed
- `string`: The text to insert

A common pattern to reset the content of an entry with a default value can be achieved with a combination of delete() and insert():

```
entry.delete(0, tk.END)
entry.insert(0, "default value")
```

Another pattern is to append the text in the current position of the text cursor. Here, you can use the INSERT constant instead of having to calculate the numerical index:

```
entry.insert(tk.INSERT, "cursor here")
```

Like the Button class, the Entry class also accepts the relief and state options to modify its border style and state. Keep in mind that calls to delete() and insert() are ignored when the state is "disabled" or "readonly".

See also

- The *Tracing text changes* recipe
- The *Validating a text entry* recipe

Tracing text changes

Tk variables allow your applications to get notified when an input changes its value. There are four variable classes in Tkinter: BooleanVar, DoubleVar, IntVar, and StringVar. Each one wraps the value of the corresponding Python type, which should match the type of the input widget attached to the variable.

This feature is particularly useful if you want to automatically update certain parts of your application based on the current state of some input widgets.

How to do it...

In the following example, we will associate a StringVar instance to our entry with the textvariable option; this variable traces write operations with the show_message() method as callback:

```
import tkinter as tk

class App(tk.Tk):
```

```
    def __init__(self):
        super().__init__()
        self.var = tk.StringVar()
        self.var.trace("w", self.show_message)
        self.entry = tk.Entry(self, textvariable=self.var)
        self.btn = tk.Button(self, text="Clear",
                            command=lambda: self.var.set(""))
        self.label = tk.Label(self)
        self.entry.pack()
        self.btn.pack()
        self.label.pack()

    def show_message(self, *args):
        value = self.var.get()
        text = "Hello, {}!".format(value) if value else ""
        self.label.config(text=text)

if __name__ == "__main__":
    app = App()
    app.mainloop()
```

When you type something into the Entry widget, the label updates its text with a message composed with the `Tk` variable value. For instance, if you type the word `Phara`, the label will show `Hello, Phara!`. If the entry is empty, the label will not show any text. To show you how to modify the variable's content programmatically, we added a button that clears the entry when you click on it:

How it works...

The first lines of our application constructor instantiate `StringVar` and attach a callback to the write mode. The valid mode values are as follows:

- `"w"`: Called when the variable is written
- `"r"`: Called when the variable is read
- `"u"` (for *unset*): Called when the variable is deleted

When invoked, the callback function receives three arguments: the internal variable name, an empty string (it is used in other types of Tk variables), and the mode that triggered the operation. By declaring the method with `*args`, we make these arguments optional, because we are not using any of these values within the callback.

The `get()` method of Tk wrappers returns the current value of the variable, and the `set()` method updates its value. They also notify the corresponding observers, so both modifying the entry's content through the GUI or clicking on the **Clear** button will trigger the call to the `show_message()` method.

There's more...

Tk variables are optional for `Entry` widgets, but they are necessary for other widget classes to work correctly, such as the `Checkbutton` and `Radiobutton` classes.

See also

- The *Creating selections with radio buttons* recipe
- The *Implementing switches with checkboxes* recipe

Validating a text entry

Typically, text inputs represent fields that follow certain validation rules, such as having a maximum length or matching a specific format. Some applications allow typing any kind of content into these fields and trigger the validation when the whole form is submitted.

Under some circumstances, we want to prevent users from typing invalid content into a text field. We will take a look at how to implement this behavior using the validation options of the Entry widget.

How to do it...

The following application shows how to validate an entry using regular expressions:

```
import re
import tkinter as tk
```

```python
class App(tk.Tk):
    def __init__(self):
        super().__init__()
        self.pattern = re.compile("^\w{0,10}$")
        self.label = tk.Label(self, text="Enter your username")
        vcmd = (self.register(self.validate_username), "%i", "%P")
        self.entry = tk.Entry(self, validate="key",
                              validatecommand=vcmd,
                              invalidcommand=self.print_error)
        self.label.pack()
        self.entry.pack(anchor=tk.W, padx=10, pady=10)

    def validate_username(self, index, username):
        print("Modification at index " + index)
        return self.pattern.match(username) is not None

    def print_error(self):
        print("Invalid username character")

if __name__ == "__main__":
    app = App()
    app.mainloop()
```

If you run this script and type a non-alphanumeric character in the Entry widget, it will keep the same content and print the error message. This will also happen when you try to type more than 10 valid characters since the regular expression also limits the content's length.

How it works...

With the `validate` option set to `"key"`, we will activate the entry validation that gets triggered on any content modification. The value is `"none"` by default, which means that there is no validation.

Other possible values are `"focusin"` and `"focusout"`, which validate when the widget gets or loses the focus, respectively, or simply `"focus"` to validate in both cases. Alternatively, we can use the `"all"` value to validate in all situations.

The `validatecommand` function is called each time the validation is triggered, and it should return `true` if the new content is valid, and `false` otherwise.

Since we need more information to determine whether the content is valid or not, we create a Tcl wrapper around our Python function using the `register` method of the `Widget` class. Then, you can add the percent substitution for each parameter that will be passed to the Python function. Finally, we will group these values as a Python tuple. This corresponds to the following line from our example:

```
vcmd = (self.register(self.validate_username), "%i", "%P")
```

In general, you can use any of the following substitutions:

- `%d`: Type of action; 1 for insertion, 0 for deletion, and -1 otherwise
- `%i`: Index of the string being inserted or deleted
- `%P`: Value of the entry if the modification is allowed
- `%s`: Value of the entry before the modification
- `%S`: String content that is being inserted or deleted
- `%v`: The type of validation currently set
- `%V`: Type of validation that triggered the action
- `%W`: The name of the Entry widget

The `invalidcommand` option takes a function that is invoked when `validatecommand` returns `false`. The same percent substitutions can be applied to this option, but in our example, we directly passed the `print_error()` method of our class.

There's more...

The Tcl/Tk documentation suggests not mixing the `validatecommand` and the `textvariable` options since setting an invalid value to the `Tk` variable will turn off validation. The same occurs if the `validatecommand` function do not return a Boolean value.

In case you are not familiar with the `re` module, you can check out the detailed introduction to regular expressions in the official Python documentation at `https://docs.python.org/3.6/howto/regex.html`.

See also

- The *Creating text entries* recipe

Selecting numerical values

Previous recipes cover how to work with text inputs; we may want to enforce some inputs to contain only numerical values. This is the use case for the Spinbox and Scale classes—both widgets allow users to select a numerical value from a range or a list of valid options, but there are several differences in the way they are displayed and configured.

How to do it...

This program has Spinbox and Scale for selecting an integer value from 0 to 5:

```python
import tkinter as tk

class App(tk.Tk):
    def __init__(self):
        super().__init__()
        self.spinbox = tk.Spinbox(self, from_=0, to=5)
        self.scale = tk.Scale(self, from_=0, to=5,
                              orient=tk.HORIZONTAL)
        self.btn = tk.Button(self, text="Print values",
                            command=self.print_values)
        self.spinbox.pack()
        self.scale.pack()
        self.btn.pack()

    def print_values(self):
        print("Spinbox: {}".format(self.spinbox.get()))
        print("Scale: {}".format(self.scale.get()))

if __name__ == "__main__":
    app = App()
    app.mainloop()
```

In the preceding code, for debugging purposes, we added a button that prints the value of each widget when you click on it:

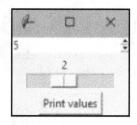

How it works...

Both classes accept the `from_` and `to` options to indicate the range of valid values—the trailing underscore is necessary because the `from` option was originally defined in Tcl/Tk, but it is a reserved keyword in Python.

A handy functionality of the `Scale` class is the `resolution` option, which sets the precision of the rounding. For instance, a resolution of 0.2 will allow the user to select the values 0.0, 0.2, 0.4, and so on. The value of this option is 1 by default, so the widget rounds all values to the nearest integer.

As usual, the value of each widget can be retrieved with the `get()` method. An important difference is that `Spinbox` returns the number as a string, whereas `Scale` returns an integer value or a float value if the rounding accepts decimal values.

There's more...

The `Spinbox` class has a similar configuration to the Entry widget, such as the `textvariable` and `validate` options. You can apply all these patterns to spinboxes with the main difference that it restricts to numerical values.

See also

- The *Tracing text changes* recipe

Creating selections with radio buttons

With the Radiobutton widget, you can let the user select among several options. This pattern works well for a relatively small number of mutually exclusive choices.

How to do it...

You can connect multiple Radiobutton instances using a Tkinter variable so that when you click on a non-selected option, it will deselect whatever other option was previously selected.

In the following program, we created three radio buttons for the Red, Green, and Blue options. Each time you click on a radio button, it prints the lowercase name of the corresponding color:

```python
import tkinter as tk

COLORS = [("Red", "red"), ("Green", "green"), ("Blue", "blue")]

class ChoiceApp(tk.Tk):
    def __init__(self):
        super().__init__()
        self.var = tk.StringVar()
        self.var.set("red")
        self.buttons = [self.create_radio(c) for c in COLORS]
        for button in self.buttons:
            button.pack(anchor=tk.W, padx=10, pady=5)

    def create_radio(self, option):
        text, value = option
        return tk.Radiobutton(self, text=text, value=value,
                              command=self.print_option,
                              variable=self.var)

    def print_option(self):
        print(self.var.get())

if __name__ == "__main__":
    app = ChoiceApp()
    app.mainloop()
```

If you run this script, it will display the application with the **Red** radio button already selected:

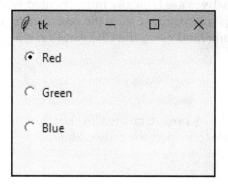

How it works...

To avoid repeating the code of the Radiobutton initialization, we defined a utility method that is called from a list comprehension. We unpacked the values of each tuple of the COLORS list and then passed these local variables as options to Radiobutton. Remember to try to not repeat yourself whenever possible.

Since StringVar is shared among all the Radiobutton instances, they are automatically connected, and we force the user to select only one choice.

There's more...

We set a default value of "red" in our program; however, what would happen if we omit this line, and the value of StringVar does not match any of the radio button values? It will match the default value of the tristatevalue option, which is the empty string. This causes the widget to display in a special "tri-state" or indeterminate mode. Although this option can be modified with the config() method, a better practice is to set a sensible default value so the variable is initialized in a valid state.

Implementing switches with checkboxes

Choices between two alternatives are typically implemented with checkboxes and lists of options where each choice is independent from the rest. As we will see in the next example, these concepts can be implemented using the Checkbutton widget.

How to do it...

The following application shows how to create Checkbutton, which must be connected to an IntVar variable to be able to inspect the button state:

```python
import tkinter as tk

class SwitchApp(tk.Tk):
    def __init__(self):
        super().__init__()
        self.var = tk.IntVar()
        self.cb = tk.Checkbutton(self, text="Active?",
                                 variable=self.var,
                                 command=self.print_value)
        self.cb.pack()

    def print_value(self):
        print(self.var.get())

if __name__ == "__main__":
    app = SwitchApp()
    app.mainloop()
```

In the preceding code, we simply printed the value of the widget each time it is clicked:

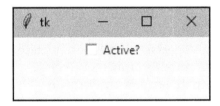

How it works...

Like the Button widget, the Checkbutton also accepts the `command` and `text` options.

With the `onvalue` and `offvalue` options, we can specify the values used when the button is on and off. We use an integer variable because these values are **1** and **0** by default, respectively; however, you can also set them to any other integer values.

There's more...

With Checkbuttons, it is also possible to use other variable types:

```
var = tk.StringVar()
var.set("OFF")
checkbutton_active = tk.Checkbutton(master, text="Active?",
variable=self.var,
                                    onvalue="ON", offvalue="OFF",
                                    command=update_value)
```

The only restriction is to match `onvalue` and `offvalue` with the type of the Tkinter variable; in this case, since "ON" and "OFF" are strings, the variable should be a `StringVar`. Otherwise, the Tcl interpreter will raise an error when trying to set the corresponding value of a different type.

See also

- The *Tracing text changes* recipe
- The *Creating selections with radio buttons* recipe

Displaying a list of items

The Listbox widget contains text items that can be selected by the user with the mouse or keyboard. This selection can be individual or multiple, depending on the widget configuration.

How to do it...

The following program creates a list selection with the days of the week. There is a button to print the actual selection and a list of buttons to change the selection mode:

```python
import tkinter as tk

DAYS = ["Monday", "Tuesday", "Wednesday", "Thursday",
        "Friday", "Saturday", "Sunday"]
MODES = [tk.SINGLE, tk.BROWSE, tk.MULTIPLE, tk.EXTENDED]

class ListApp(tk.Tk):
    def __init__(self):
        super().__init__()
        self.list = tk.Listbox(self)
        self.list.insert(0, *DAYS)
        self.print_btn = tk.Button(self, text="Print selection",
                                   command=self.print_selection)
        self.btns = [self.create_btn(m) for m in MODES]

        self.list.pack()
        self.print_btn.pack(fill=tk.BOTH)
        for btn in self.btns:
            btn.pack(side=tk.LEFT)

    def create_btn(self, mode):
        cmd = lambda: self.list.config(selectmode=mode)
        return tk.Button(self, command=cmd,
                         text=mode.capitalize())

    def print_selection(self):
        selection = self.list.curselection()
        print([self.list.get(i) for i in selection])

if __name__ == "__main__":
    app = ListApp()
    app.mainloop()
```

You can try out changing the mode of selection and printing the selected items:

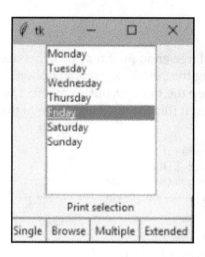

How it works...

We create an empty Listbox object and add all the text items with the `insert()` method. The 0 index indicates that the items should be added at the beginning of the list. In the following code snippet, we unpacked the DAYS list, but individual items can be appended at the end with the END constant:

```
self.list.insert(tk.END, "New item")
```

The current selection is retrieved using the `curselection()` method. It returns the indices of the selected items to transform them to the corresponding text items we called the `get()` method for each index in a comprehension list. Finally, the list is printed in the standard output for debugging purposes.

In our example, the `selectmode` option can be changed programmatically to explore the different behaviors, as follows:

- SINGLE: Single choice
- BROWSE: Single choice that can be moved with the up and down keys
- MULTIPLE: Multiple choice
- EXTENDED: Multiple choice with ranges that can be selected with the *Shift* and *Ctrl* keys

There's more...

If the number of text items is large enough, it may be necessary to add a vertical scroll bar. You can easily connect it using the `yscrollcommand` option. In our example, we can wrap both widgets in a frame to keep the same layout. Remember to specify the `fill` option when packing the scroll so that it fills the available space in the *y* axis:

```python
def __init__(self):
    self.frame = tk.Frame(self)
    self.scroll = tk.Scrollbar(self.frame, orient=tk.VERTICAL)
    self.list = tk.Listbox(self.frame, yscrollcommand=self.scroll.set)
    self.scroll.config(command=self.list.yview)
    # ...
    self.frame.pack()
    self.list.pack(side=tk.LEFT)
    self.scroll.pack(side=tk.LEFT, fill=tk.Y)
```

Similarly, there is a `xscrollcommand` option for the horizontal axis.

See also

- The *Creating selections with radio buttons* recipe

Handling mouse and keyboard events

Being able to react to events is one of the most basic but important topics in GUI application development since it determines how users can interact with the program.

Pressing keys of the keyboard and clicking on items with the mouse are some common types of events, which are automatically handled in some Tkinter classes. For instance, this behavior is already implemented on the `command` option of the `Button` widget class, which invokes the specified callback function.

Some events can get triggered without user interaction, such as changing the input focus programmatically from one widget to another.

How to do it...

You can attach an event binding to a widget using the `bind` method. The following example binds some mouse events to a `Frame` instance:

```python
import tkinter as tk

class App(tk.Tk):
    def __init__(self):
        super().__init__()
        frame = tk.Frame(self, bg="green",
                         height=100, width=100)
        frame.bind("<Button-1>", self.print_event)
        frame.bind("<Double-Button-1>", self.print_event)
        frame.bind("<ButtonRelease-1>", self.print_event)
        frame.bind("<B1-Motion>", self.print_event)
        frame.bind("<Enter>", self.print_event)
        frame.bind("<Leave>", self.print_event)
        frame.pack(padx=50, pady=50)

    def print_event(self, event):
        position = "(x={}, y={})".format(event.x, event.y)
        print(event.type, "event", position)

if __name__ == "__main__":
    app = App()
    app.mainloop()
```

All events are handled by the `print_event()` method of our class, which prints the type of event and the position of the mouse in the console. You can try it out by clicking on the green frame with the mouse, and moving it around while it starts printing the event messages.

The following example contains an Entry widget with a couple of bindings; one for the event that gets triggered when the entry gets the focus, and another for all the key press events:

```python
import tkinter as tk

class App(tk.Tk):
    def __init__(self):
        super().__init__()
        entry = tk.Entry(self)
        entry.bind("<FocusIn>", self.print_type)
        entry.bind("<Key>", self.print_key)
        entry.pack(padx=20, pady=20)
```

```
    def print_type(self, event):
        print(event.type)

    def print_key(self, event):
        args = event.keysym, event.keycode, event.char
        print("Symbol: {}, Code: {}, Char: {}".format(*args))

if __name__ == "__main__":
    app = App()
    app.mainloop()
```

The first message this program will output is the `FocusIn` event when you set the focus on the Entry widget. If you try it out, you will see that it will also show the events of keys that do not correspond to non-printable characters, such as arrow keys or the return key.

How it works...

The `bind` method is defined in the `widget` class and takes three arguments, an event sequence, a `callback` function, and an optional `add` string:

```
widget.bind(sequence, callback, add='')
```

The `sequence` string uses the `<modifier-type-detail>` syntax.

In first place, modifiers are optional and allow you to specify additional combinations to the general type of the event:

- `Shift`: When the user presses the *Shift* key
- `Alt`: When the user presses the *Alt* key
- `Control`: When the user presses the *Ctrl* key
- `Lock`: When the user presses the *Shift* lock
- `Double`: When the event happens twice in quick succession
- `Triple`: When the event happens thrice in quick succession

Event types determine the general type of event:

- `ButtonPress` or `Button`: Event generated when a mouse button is pressed
- `ButtonRelease`: Event generated when a mouse button is released
- `Enter`: Event generated when you move the mouse over a widget
- `Leave`: Event generated when the mouse pointer leaves a widget

- `FocusIn`: Event generated when the widget gets the input focus
- `FocusOut`: Event generated when the widget loses the input focus
- `KeyPress` or `Key`: Event generated when a key is pressed
- `KeyRelease`: Event generated when a key is released
- `Motion`: Event generated when the mouse is moved

The detail is also optional and serves to indicate the mouse button or key:

- For mouse events, 1 is the left button, 2 is the middle button, and 3 is the right button.
- For keyboard events, it is the key character. Special keys use the key symbol; some common examples are return, *Tab*, *Esc*, up, down, right, left, *Backspace*, and function keys (from *F1* to *F12*).

The `callback` function takes an event parameter. For mouse events, it has the following attributes:

- `x` and `y`: Current mouse position in pixels
- `x_root` and `y_root`: Same as `x` and `y`, but relative to the left-upper corner of the screen
- `num`: Mouse button number

For keyboard events, it contains these attributes:

- `char`: Pressed character code as a string
- `keysym`: Pressed key symbol
- `keycode`: Pressed key code

In both cases, the event has the `widget` attribute, referencing the instance that generated the event, and `type`, which specifies the event type.

> We strongly recommend that you define methods for the `callback` functions since you will also have the reference to the class instance, and therefore you can easily access each of the `widget` attributes.

Finally, the `add` parameter can be `' '`, to replace the `callback` function if there was a previous binding, or `'+'` to add the callback and preserve the old ones.

There's more...

Apart from the event types described here, there are also other types that may be useful in some scenarios, such as the <Destroy> event that is generated when a widget is destroyed or the <Configure> event that is sent when the size or position of the widget changes.

You can check out the Tcl/Tk documentation for a complete list of event types at https://www.tcl.tk/man/tcl/TkCmd/bind.htm#M7.

See also

- The *Structuring a Tkinter application* recipe

Setting the main window's icon, title, and size

The Tk instance differs from normal widgets in the way that it is configured, so we will explore some basic methods that allow us to customize how it is displayed.

How to do it...

This snippet creates a main window with a custom title and icon. It has 400px of width by 200px of height, with a separation of 10px in each axis to the upper-left corner of the screen:

```python
import tkinter as tk

class App(tk.Tk):
    def __init__(self):
        super().__init__()
        self.title("My Tkinter app")
        self.iconbitmap("python.ico")
        self.geometry("400x200+10+10")

if __name__ == "__main__":
    app = App()
    app.mainloop()
```

This program assumes that you have a valid ICO file called `python.ico` in the same directory where the script is placed and executed.

How it works...

The methods `title()` and `iconbitmap()` of the `Tk` class are very self-descriptive—the first one sets the window title, whereas the second one takes the path to the icon that is associated to the window.

The `geometry()` method configures the size of the window with a string that follows the following pattern:

{width}x{height}+{offset_x}+{offset_y}

In case you add more secondary windows to your application, these methods are also available in the `Toplevel` class.

There's more...

If you want to make the application fullscreen, replace the call to the `geometry()` method with `self.state("zoomed")`.

Window Layout

2

In this chapter, we will cover the following recipes:

- Grouping widgets with frames
- Using the Pack geometry manager
- Using the Grid geometry manager
- Using the Place geometry manager
- Grouping inputs with the FrameLabel widget
- Dynamically laying out widgets
- Creating horizontal and vertical scrollbars

Introduction

Widgets determine the actions that users can perform with our GUI application; however, we should pay attention to their placement and the relationships we establish with that arrangement. Effective layouts help users to identify the meaning and priority of each graphical element so that they can quickly understand how to interact with our program.

Layout also determines the visual appearance that users expect to find consistently across the whole application, such as always placing confirmation buttons at the bottom-right corner of the screen. Although this information might be obvious to us as developers, end users may feel overwhelmed if we do not guide them through the application by following a natural order.

This chapter will dive into the different mechanisms that Tkinter offers to lay out and group widgets and control other attributes, such as their size or spacing.

Grouping widgets with frames

A frame represents a rectangular region of a window, typically used in complex layouts to contain other widgets. Since they have their own padding, border, and background, you can remark that the group of widgets is related logically.

Another common pattern for frames is to encapsulate part of the application's functionality so that you can create an abstraction that hides the implementation details of child widgets.

We will see an example that covers both scenarios by creating a component that inherits from the Frame class and exposes certain information on the containing widgets.

Getting ready

We will build an application that contains two lists, where the first one has a list of items and the second one is initially empty. Both lists are scrollable, and you can move items between them with two central buttons that transfer the current selection:

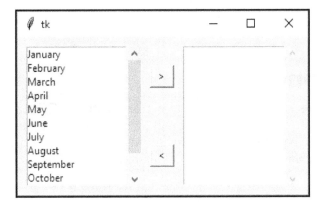

How to do it...

We will define a Frame subclass to represent a scrollable list, and then create two instances of this class. The two buttons will also be directly added to the main window:

```
import tkinter as tk

class ListFrame(tk.Frame):
    def __init__(self, master, items=[]):
        super().__init__(master)
```

```python
        self.list = tk.Listbox(self)
        self.scroll = tk.Scrollbar(self, orient=tk.VERTICAL,
                                   command=self.list.yview)
        self.list.config(yscrollcommand=self.scroll.set)
        self.list.insert(0, *items)
        self.list.pack(side=tk.LEFT)
        self.scroll.pack(side=tk.LEFT, fill=tk.Y)


    def pop_selection(self):
        index = self.list.curselection()
        if index:
            value = self.list.get(index)
            self.list.delete(index)
            return value

    def insert_item(self, item):
        self.list.insert(tk.END, item)

class App(tk.Tk):
    def __init__(self):
        super().__init__()
        months = ["January", "February", "March", "April",
                  "May", "June", "July", "August", "September",
                  "October", "November", "December"]
        self.frame_a = ListFrame(self, months)
        self.frame_b = ListFrame(self)
        self.btn_right = tk.Button(self, text=">",
                                   command=self.move_right)
        self.btn_left = tk.Button(self, text="<",
                                  command=self.move_left)

        self.frame_a.pack(side=tk.LEFT, padx=10, pady=10)
        self.frame_b.pack(side=tk.RIGHT, padx=10, pady=10)
        self.btn_right.pack(expand=True, ipadx=5)
        self.btn_left.pack(expand=True, ipadx=5)

    def move_right(self):
        self.move(self.frame_a, self.frame_b)

    def move_left(self):
        self.move(self.frame_b, self.frame_a)

    def move(self, frame_from, frame_to):
        value = frame_from.pop_selection()
        if value:
            frame_to.insert_item(value)
```

```
if __name__ == "__main__":
    app = App()
    app.mainloop()
```

How it works...

Our `ListFrame` class has only two methods to interact with the inner list: `pop_selection()` and `insert_item()`. The first one returns and deletes the current selection, or none if there is no item selected, whereas the second one inserts a new item at the end of the list.

These methods are used in the parent class to transfer an item from one list to the other one:

```
def move(self, frame_from, frame_to):
    value = frame_from.pop_selection()
    if value:
        frame_to.insert_item(value)
```

We also took advantage of the parent frame containers to correctly pack them with the appropriate padding:

```
# ...
self.frame_a.pack(side=tk.LEFT, padx=10, pady=10)
self.frame_b.pack(side=tk.RIGHT, padx=10, pady=10)
```

Thanks to these frames, our calls to the geometry manager are more isolated and organized in our global layout.

There's more...

Another benefit of this approach is that it allows us to use different geometry managers in each container widget, such as using `grid()` for the widgets within a frame and `pack()` to lay out the frame in the main window.

However, remember that mixing these geometry managers within the same container is not allowed in Tkinter and will make your application crash.

See also

- The *Using the Pack geometry manager* recipe

Using the Pack geometry manager

In previous recipes, we have seen that creating a widget does not automatically display it on the screen. We have called the `pack()` method on each widget to do so, which means that we used the Pack geometry manager.

This is one of the three available geometry managers in Tkinter, and it is well suited for simple layouts, such as when you want to place all the widgets on top of each other or side by side.

Getting ready

Let's suppose that we want to achieve the following layout in our application:

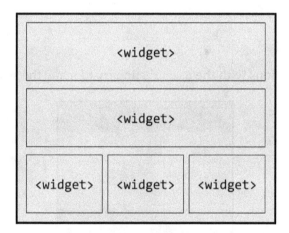

It consists of three rows, where the last one has three widgets placed side by side. In this scenario, the Pack geometry manager can easily add the widgets as expected, without the need for additional frames.

How to do it...

We will use five Label widgets with different texts and background colors to help us identify each rectangular region:

```
import tkinter as tk

class App(tk.Tk):
    def __init__(self):
        super().__init__()
        label_a = tk.Label(self, text="Label A", bg="yellow")
        label_b = tk.Label(self, text="Label B", bg="orange")
        label_c = tk.Label(self, text="Label C", bg="red")
        label_d = tk.Label(self, text="Label D", bg="green")
        label_e = tk.Label(self, text="Label E", bg="blue")

        opts = { 'ipadx': 10, 'ipady': 10, 'fill': tk.BOTH }
        label_a.pack(side=tk.TOP, **opts)
        label_b.pack(side=tk.TOP, **opts)
        label_c.pack(side=tk.LEFT, **opts)
        label_d.pack(side=tk.LEFT, **opts)
        label_e.pack(side=tk.LEFT, **opts)

if __name__ == "__main__":
    app = App()
    app.mainloop()
```

We also added some options with the opts dictionary to make the size of each region clear:

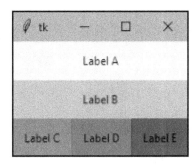

How it works...

To have a better understanding of the Pack geometry manager, we will explain step by step how it adds widgets to the parent container. Here, we pay special attention to the values of the side option, which indicates, the relative position of the widget with respect to the next one that will be packed.

First, we pack the two labels at the top of the screen. While the tk.TOP constant is the default value of the side option, we set it explicitly to clearly differentiate it from the calls where we used the tk.LEFT value:

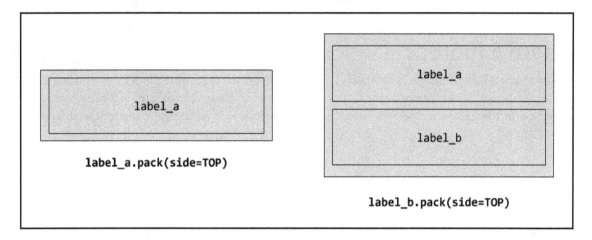

Then, we pack the next three labels with the side option set to tk.LEFT, which causes them to be placed side by side:

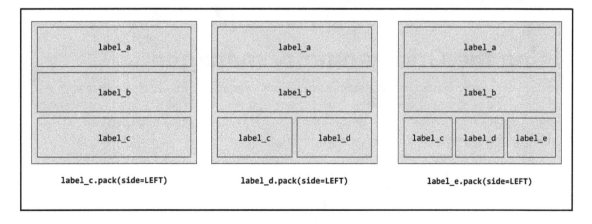

Specifying the side on `label_e` does not really matter, as long as it is the last widget we add to the container.

Keep in mind that this is the reason why order is so important when working with the Pack geometry manager. To prevent unexpected results in complex layouts, it is common to group widgets with frames so that when you pack all the widgets within a frame, you do not interfere with the arrangement of the other ones.

In these cases, we strongly recommend that you use the Grid geometry manager since it allows you to directly set the position of each widget with one call to the geometry manager and avoids the need for additional frames.

There's more...

Apart from `tk.TOP` and `tk.LEFT`, you can pass the `tk.BOTTOM` and `tk.RIGHT` constants to the `side` option. They perform the opposite stacking, as their names suggest; however, it may be counterintuitive since the natural order we follow is from top to bottom and from left to right.

For instance, if we replace the `tk.LEFT` value with `tk.RIGHT` in our three last widgets, their order from left to right would be `label_e`, `label_d`, and `label_c`.

See also

- The *Using the Grid geometry manager* recipe
- The *Using the Place geometry manager* recipe

Using the Grid geometry manager

The Grid geometry manager is considered the more versatile of the three geometry managers. It directly reassembles the *grid* concept that is commonly used in user interface design—a two-dimensional table divided into rows and columns, where each cell represents the space available for a widget.

Getting ready

We will demonstrate how to use the Grid geometry manager to achieve the following
layout:

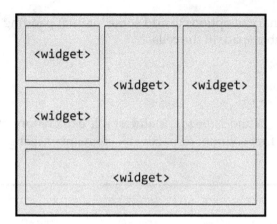

This can be represented as a 3 x 3 table, where the widgets in the second and third columns
span two rows and the widget at the bottom row spans three columns.

How to do it...

As we did in the preceding recipe, we will use five labels with different backgrounds to
illustrate the distribution of the cells:

```
import tkinter as tk

class App(tk.Tk):
    def __init__(self):
        super().__init__()
        label_a = tk.Label(self, text="Label A", bg="yellow")
        label_b = tk.Label(self, text="Label B", bg="orange")
        label_c = tk.Label(self, text="Label C", bg="red")
        label_d = tk.Label(self, text="Label D", bg="green")
        label_e = tk.Label(self, text="Label E", bg="blue")

        opts = { 'ipadx': 10, 'ipady': 10 , 'sticky': 'nswe' }
        label_a.grid(row=0, column=0, **opts)
        label_b.grid(row=1, column=0, **opts)
        label_c.grid(row=0, column=1, rowspan=2, **opts)
        label_d.grid(row=0, column=2, rowspan=2, **opts)
```

```
            label_e.grid(row=2, column=0, columnspan=3, **opts)

    if __name__ == "__main__":
        app = App()
        app.mainloop()
```

We also passed a dictionary of options to add some internal padding and expand the widgets to all the available space in the cells.

How it works...

The placement of label_a and label_b is almost self-explanatory: they occupy the first and second rows of the first column, respectively—remember that grid positions are zero-indexed:

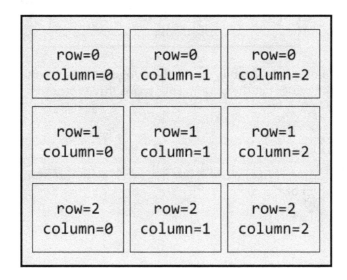

To expand label_c and label_d through multiple cells, we will set the rowspan option to 2, so they will span two cells, starting from the position indicated with the row and column options. Finally, we will place label_e with the columnspan option to set it to 3.

It is important to remark that in contrast with the Pack geometry manager, it is possible to change the order of the calls to grid() on each widget without modifying the final layout.

There's more...

The `sticky` option indicates the borders where the widget should stick, expressed in cardinal directions: north, south, west and east. These values are represented by the Tkinter constants `tk.N`, `tk.S`, `tk.W`, and `tk.E`, as well as the combined versions `tk.NW`, `tk.NE`, `tk.SW`, and `tk.SE`.

For example, `sticky=tk.N` aligns the widget to the top border of the cell (north), whereas `sticky=tk.SE` positions the widget in the bottom-right corner of the cell (south-east).

Since these constants represent their corresponding lowercase letters, we shorthanded the `tk.N + tk.S + tk.W + tk.E` expression with the `"nswe"` string. This means that the widget should expand both horizontally and vertically—similar to the `fill=tk.BOTH` option of the Pack geometry manager.

If no value is passed to the `sticky` option, the widget is centered within the cell.

See also

- The *Using the Pack geometry manager* recipe
- The *Using the Place geometry manager* recipe

Using the Place geometry manager

The Place geometry manager allows you to set the position and size of a widget in absolute terms, or in relative terms to another one.

Of the three geometry managers, it is the least commonly used one. On the other hand, it can fit some complex scenarios where you want to freely position a widget or overlap a previously placed one.

Getting ready

To demonstrate how to work with the Place geometry manager, we will replicate the following layout by mixing absolute and relative positions and sizes:

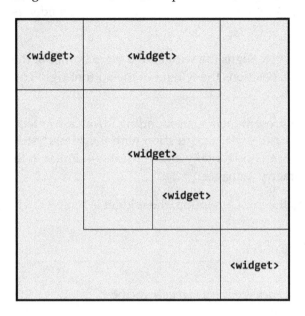

How to do it...

The labels that we will display have different backgrounds and are defined in the order they are placed from left to right and top to bottom:

```
import tkinter as tk

class App(tk.Tk):
    def __init__(self):
        super().__init__()
        label_a = tk.Label(self, text="Label A", bg="yellow")
        label_b = tk.Label(self, text="Label B", bg="orange")
        label_c = tk.Label(self, text="Label C", bg="red")
        label_d = tk.Label(self, text="Label D", bg="green")
        label_e = tk.Label(self, text="Label E", bg="blue")

        label_a.place(relwidth=0.25, relheight=0.25)
        label_b.place(x=100, anchor=tk.N,
                      width=100, height=50)
```

```
        label_c.place(relx=0.5, rely=0.5, anchor=tk.CENTER,
                      relwidth=0.5, relheight=0.5)
        label_d.place(in_=label_c, anchor=tk.N + tk.W,
                      x=2, y=2, relx=0.5, rely=0.5,
                      relwidth=0.5, relheight=0.5)
        label_e.place(x=200, y=200, anchor=tk.S + tk.E,
                      relwidth=0.25, relheight=0.25)

if __name__ == "__main__":
    app = App()
    app.mainloop()
```

If you run the preceding program, you can see the overlapping between `label_c` and `label_d` in the center of the screen, something that we have not achieved with other geometry managers.

How it works...

The first label is placed with the `relwidth` and `relheight` options set to 0.25, which means that its width and height are 25% of its parent container. By default, widgets are placed at the x=0 and y=0 positions and aligned to north-west, that is, the top-left corner of the screen.

The second label is placed at the absolute position—x=100—and aligned to the top border with the `anchor` option set to the `tk.N` (north) constant. Here, we also specified an absolute size with `width` and `height`.

The third label is centered on the window using the relative positioning and setting the `anchor` to `tk.CENTER`. Remember that a value of 0.5 for `relx` and `relwidth` means half of the parent's width and a value of 0.5 for `rely`, and `relheight` means half of the parent's height.

The fourth label is placed on top of `label_c` by passing it as the `in_` argument (note that Tkinter suffixes it with an underscore because `in` is a reserved keyword). When using `in_`, you might notice that the alignment is not geometrically exact. In our example, we had to add an offset of 2 pixels in each direction to perfectly overlap the right-bottom corner of `label_c`.

Finally, the fifth label uses absolute positioning and relative size. As you may have already noticed, these dimensions can be easily switched since we assume a parent container of 200 x 200 pixels; however, only relative weights will work as expected if the main window is resized. You can test this behavior by resizing the window.

There's more...

Another important advantage of the Place geometry manager is that it may be used in conjunction with Pack or Grid.

For instance, imagine that you want to dynamically display a caption over a widget when you right-click on it. You can represent this caption with a Label widget, which gets placed in the relative position where you clicked on the widget:

```
def show_caption(self, event):
    caption = tk.Label(self, ...)
    caption.place(in_=event.widget, x=event.x, y=event.y)
    # ...
```

As general advice, we recommend that you use any of the other geometry managers as much as possible in your Tkinter applications and leave this only for those specialized cases where you need a custom positioning.

See also

- The *Using the Pack geometry manager* recipe
- The *Using the Grid geometry manager* recipe

Grouping inputs with the LabelFrame widget

The LabelFrame class can be used to group multiple input widgets, indicating the logical entity with a label they represent. It is typically used in forms and is very similar to the Frame widget.

Getting ready

We will build a form with a couple of LabelFrame instances, each one with their corresponding child input widgets:

How to do it...

Since the purpose of this example is to show the final layout, we will add some widgets, without keeping their references as attributes:

```python
import tkinter as tk

class App(tk.Tk):
    def __init__(self):
        super().__init__()
        group_1 = tk.LabelFrame(self, padx=15, pady=10,
                                text="Personal Information")
        group_1.pack(padx=10, pady=5)

        tk.Label(group_1, text="First name").grid(row=0)
        tk.Label(group_1, text="Last name").grid(row=1)
        tk.Entry(group_1).grid(row=0, column=1, sticky=tk.W)
        tk.Entry(group_1).grid(row=1, column=1, sticky=tk.W)

        group_2 = tk.LabelFrame(self, padx=15, pady=10,
                                text="Address")
        group_2.pack(padx=10, pady=5)

        tk.Label(group_2, text="Street").grid(row=0)
        tk.Label(group_2, text="City").grid(row=1)
```

```
        tk.Label(group_2, text="ZIP Code").grid(row=2)
        tk.Entry(group_2).grid(row=0, column=1, sticky=tk.W)
        tk.Entry(group_2).grid(row=1, column=1, sticky=tk.W)
        tk.Entry(group_2, width=8).grid(row=2, column=1,
                                        sticky=tk.W)

        self.btn_submit = tk.Button(self, text="Submit")
        self.btn_submit.pack(padx=10, pady=10, side=tk.RIGHT)

if __name__ == "__main__":
    app = App()
    app.mainloop()
```

How it works...

The LabelFrame widget takes the labelwidget option to set the widget used as a label. If it is not present, it displays the string passed as the text option. For instance, instead of creating an instance with tk.LabelFrame(master, text="Info"), you can replace it with the following statements:

```
label = tk.Label(master, text="Info", ...)
frame = tk.LabelFrame(master, labelwidget=label)
# ...
frame.pack()
```

This would allow you to do any kind of customization, such as adding an image. Note that we did not use any geometry manager for the label since it is managed when you place the frame.

Dynamically laying out widgets

The Grid geometry manager is easy to use both in simple and advanced layouts, and it is also a powerful mechanism to combine with a list of widgets.

We will take a look at how we can reduce the number of lines and call the geometry manager methods with just a few lines, thanks to list comprehensions and the zip and enumerate built-in functions.

Getting ready

The application we will build contains four Entry widgets, each one with its corresponding label that indicates the meaning of the input. We will also add a button to print all the entries' values:

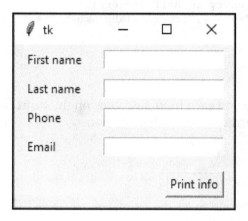

Instead of creating and assigning each widget to a separate attribute, we will work with lists of widgets. Since we will track the index while iterating over these lists, we can easily invoke the grid() method with the appropriate column option.

How to do it...

We will aggregate the lists of labels and entries with the zip function. The button will be created and displayed individually, as it does not share any option with the rest of the widgets:

```
import tkinter as tk

class App(tk.Tk):
    def __init__(self):
        super().__init__()
        fields = ["First name", "Last name", "Phone", "Email"]
        labels = [tk.Label(self, text=f) for f in fields]
        entries = [tk.Entry(self) for _ in fields]
        self.widgets = list(zip(labels, entries))
        self.submit = tk.Button(self, text="Print info",
                                command=self.print_info)

        for i, (label, entry) in enumerate(self.widgets):
```

```
                label.grid(row=i, column=0, padx=10, sticky=tk.W)
                entry.grid(row=i, column=1, padx=10, pady=5)
        self.submit.grid(row=len(fields), column=1, sticky=tk.E,
                         padx=10, pady=10)

    def print_info(self):
        for label, entry in self.widgets:
            print("{} = {}".format(label.cget("text"), "=", entry.get()))

if __name__ == "__main__":
    app = App()
    app.mainloop()
```

You can enter different text on each input and click on the **Print info** button to verify that each tuple contains the corresponding label and entry.

How it works...

Each list comprehension iterates over the strings of the fields list. While labels use each item as the displayed text, entries only need the reference to the parent container—the underscore is a common idiom that means the variable value is ignored.

Starting from Python 3, zip returns an iterator instead of a list, so we consume the aggregation with the list function. As a result, the widgets attribute contains a list of tuples that can be safely iterated multiple times:

```
fields = ["First name", "Last name", "Phone", "Email"]
labels = [tk.Label(self, text=f) for f in fields]
entries = [tk.Entry(self) for _ in fields]
self.widgets = list(zip(labels, entries))
```

Now, we have to call the geometry manager on each tuple of widgets. With the enumerate function, we can track the index of each iteration and pass it as the *row* number:

```
for i, (label, entry) in enumerate(self.widgets):
    label.grid(row=i, column=0, padx=10, sticky=tk.W)
    entry.grid(row=i, column=1, padx=10, pady=5)
```

Note that we used the for i, (label, entry) in ... syntax because we must unpack the tuple generated with enumerate, and then unpack each tuple of the widgets attribute.

Within the print_info() callback, we iterate over widgets to print each label text with its corresponding entry value. To retrieve the labels' text, we used the cget() method, which allows you to get the value of a widget option by its name.

Creating horizontal and vertical scrollbars

In Tkinter, geometry managers take all the necessary space to fit all the widgets in their parent container. However, if the container has a fixed size or exceeds the screen's size, there will be a region that will not be visible to users.

Scroll bar widgets are not automatically added in Tkinter, so you must create and lay them out as any other type of widget. Another consideration is that only a few widget classes have the configuration options that make it possible to connect them to a scrollbar.

To work around this, you will learn to take advantage of the flexibility of the **Canvas** widget to make any container scrollable.

Getting ready

To demonstrate the combination of the Canvas and Scrollbar classes to create a resizable and scrollable frame, we will build an application that dynamically changes its size by loading an image.

When the **Load image** button is clicked, it removes itself and loads an image into the Canvas that is larger than the scrollable region—for this example, we used a predefined image, but you can modify this program to select any other GIF image with a file dialog:

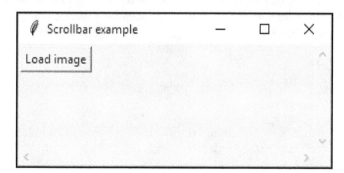

This enables the horizontal and vertical scrollbars, which automatically adjust themselves if the main window is resized:

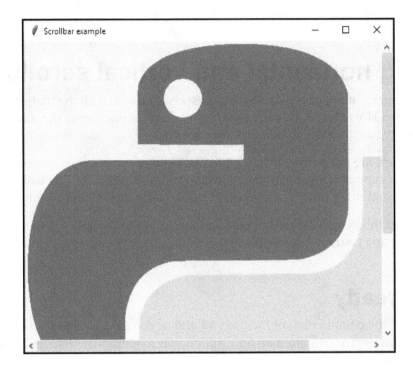

How to do it...

When we will dive into the functionality of the Canvas widget in a separate chapter, this application will introduce its standard scroll interface and the `create_window()` method. Note that this script requires the file `python.gif` to be placed in the same directory:

```python
import tkinter as tk

class App(tk.Tk):
    def __init__(self):
        super().__init__()
        self.scroll_x = tk.Scrollbar(self, orient=tk.HORIZONTAL)
        self.scroll_y = tk.Scrollbar(self, orient=tk.VERTICAL)
        self.canvas = tk.Canvas(self, width=300, height=100,
                                xscrollcommand=self.scroll_x.set,
                                yscrollcommand=self.scroll_y.set)
        self.scroll_x.config(command=self.canvas.xview)
```

```
        self.scroll_y.config(command=self.canvas.yview)

        self.frame = tk.Frame(self.canvas)
        self.btn = tk.Button(self.frame, text="Load image",
                            command=self.load_image)
        self.btn.pack()

        self.canvas.create_window((0, 0), window=self.frame,
                                    anchor=tk.NW)

        self.canvas.grid(row=0, column=0, sticky="nswe")
        self.scroll_x.grid(row=1, column=0, sticky="we")
        self.scroll_y.grid(row=0, column=1, sticky="ns")

        self.rowconfigure(0, weight=1)
        self.columnconfigure(0, weight=1)
        self.bind("<Configure>", self.resize)
        self.update_idletasks()
        self.minsize(self.winfo_width(), self.winfo_height())

    def resize(self, event):
        region = self.canvas.bbox(tk.ALL)
        self.canvas.configure(scrollregion=region)

    def load_image(self):
        self.btn.destroy()
        self.image = tk.PhotoImage(file="python.gif")
        tk.Label(self.frame, image=self.image).pack()

if __name__ == "__main__":
    app = App()
    app.mainloop()
```

How it works...

The first lines of our application create the scroll bars and connect them to
the `Canvas` object with the `xscrollcommand` and `yscrollcommand` options, which take a
reference to the `set()` method of `scroll_x` and `scroll_y`, respectively—this is the
method in charge of moving the scroll bar slider.

It is also necessary to configure the `command` option of each scroll bar once the `Canvas` is
defined:

```
    self.scroll_x = tk.Scrollbar(self, orient=tk.HORIZONTAL)
    self.scroll_y = tk.Scrollbar(self, orient=tk.VERTICAL)
```

```
self.canvas = tk.Canvas(self, width=300, height=100,
                        xscrollcommand=self.scroll_x.set,
                        yscrollcommand=self.scroll_y.set)
self.scroll_x.config(command=self.canvas.xview)
self.scroll_y.config(command=self.canvas.yview)
```

It is also possible to create the `Canvas` first and configure its options later, when the scroll bars are instantiated.

The next step is to add the frame to our scrollable `Canvas` with the `create_window()` method. The first argument it takes is the position to place the widget passed with the `window` option. Since the *x* and *y* axes of the `Canvas` widget start in the top-left corner, we placed the frame at the `(0, 0)` position and also aligned it to that corner with `anchor=tk.NW` (north-west):

```
self.frame = tk.Frame(self.canvas)
# ...
self.canvas.create_window((0, 0), window=self.frame, anchor=tk.NW)
```

Then, we will make the first row and column resizable with the `rowconfigure()` and `columnconfigure()` methods. The `weight` option indicates the relative weight to distribute the extra space, but in our case, there are no more rows or columns to resize.

The binding to the `<Configure>` event will help us to properly reconfigure the `canvas` when the main window gets resized. Handling this type of event follows the same principles that we saw in the previous chapter to process mouse and keyboard events:

```
self.rowconfigure(0, weight=1)
self.columnconfigure(0, weight=1)
self.bind("<Configure>", self.resize)
```

Finally, we will set the minimum size of the main window with the current width and height, which can be retrieved with the `winfo_width()` and `winfo_height()` methods.

In order to get the real size of a container, we have to force the geometry manager to draw all the child widgets first by calling `update_idletasks()`. This method is available in all widget classes, and forces Tkinter to process all pending idle events, such as redrawings and geometry recalculations:

```
self.update_idletasks()
self.minsize(self.winfo_width(), self.winfo_height())
```

The `resize` method handles the window resize event and updates the `scrollregion` option, which defines the area of the `canvas` that can be scrolled. To easily recalculate it, you can use the `bbox()` method with the `ALL` constant. This returns the bounding box of the whole Canvas widget:

```
def resize(self, event):
    region = self.canvas.bbox(tk.ALL)
    self.canvas.configure(scrollregion=region)
```

Tkinter will automatically trigger several `<Configure>` events when we start our application, so there is no need to call `self.resize()` at the end of the __init__ method.

There's more...

Only a few widget classes support the standard scroll options: `Listbox`, `Text`, and `Canvas` allow `xscrollcommand` and `yscrollcommand`, whereas the Entry widget only allows the `xscrollcommand`. We have seen how to apply this pattern to a `canvas` since it can be used as a generic solution, but you can follow a similar structure to make any of these widgets scrollable and resizable.

Another detail to point out is that we did not call any geometry manager to draw the frame because the `create_window()` method does this for us. To better organize our application class, we could move all the functionalities that belong to the frame and its inner widgets to a dedicated `Frame` subclass.

See also

- The *Handling mouse and keyboard events* recipe
- The *Grouping widgets with frames* recipe

Customizing Widgets **3**

In this chapter, we will cover the following recipes:

- Working with colors
- Setting widget fonts
- Using the options database
- Changing the cursor icon
- Introducing the Text widget
- Adding tags to the Text widget

Introduction

By default, Tkinter widgets will display with a native look and feel. While this standard appearance could be enough for quick prototyping, we might want to customize some widget attributes, such as font, color, and background.

This customization does not affect only the widgets itself, but also its inner items. We will dive into the Text widget, which along with the Canvas widget is one of the most versatile Tkinter classes. The Text widget represents a multiline text area with formatted content, with several methods that make it possible to format characters or lines and add event-specific event bindings.

Working with colors

In previous recipes, we have set the colors of a widget using color names, such as white, blue, or yellow. These values are passed as strings to the `foreground` and `background` options, which modify the widget's text and background colors.

Color names are internally mapped to **RGB** values (an additive model that represents a color by its combination of red, green, and blue intensities), and this translation is based on a table that is platform-dependent. Therefore, if you want to consistently display the same color in different platforms, you can pass the RGB value to the widget options.

Getting ready

The following application shows how to dynamically change the `foreground` and `background` options of a label that displays a fixed text:

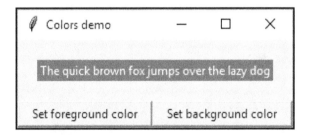

Colors are specified in the RGB format and are selected by the user using a native color picker dialog. The following screenshot shows how this dialog looks on Windows 10:

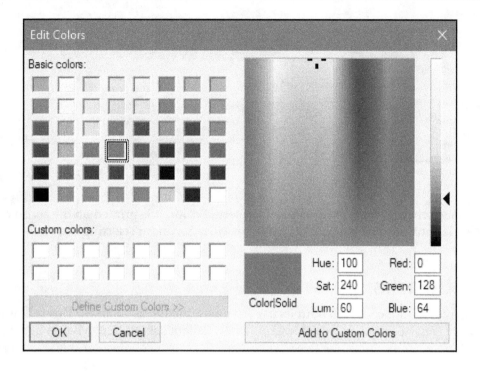

How to do it...

As usual, we will trigger the widget configuration with standard buttons—one for each option. The main difference with previous examples is that values can be directly chosen using the `askcolor` dialog from the `tkinter.colorchooser` module:

```python
from functools import partial

import tkinter as tk
from tkinter.colorchooser import askcolor

class App(tk.Tk):
    def __init__(self):
        super().__init__()
        self.title("Colors demo")
        text = "The quick brown fox jumps over the lazy dog"
        self.label = tk.Label(self, text=text)
        self.fg_btn = tk.Button(self, text="Set foreground color",
                                command=partial(self.set_color, "fg"))
        self.bg_btn = tk.Button(self, text="Set background color",
                                command=partial(self.set_color, "bg"))
```

```
        self.label.pack(padx=20, pady=20)
        self.fg_btn.pack(side=tk.LEFT, fill=tk.BOTH, expand=True)
        self.bg_btn.pack(side=tk.LEFT, fill=tk.BOTH, expand=True)

    def set_color(self, option):
        color = askcolor()[1]
        print("Chosen color:", color)
        self.label.config(**{option: color})

if __name__ == "__main__":
    app = App()
    app.mainloop()
```

If you want to check out the RGB value of a selected color, it is printed on the console when the dialog is confirmed, or none is shown if it is closed without selecting a color.

How it works...

As you may have noticed, both buttons use a partial function as callback. This is a utility from the `functools` module, which creates a new callable object that behaves like the original function, but with some fixed arguments. For instance, consider this statement:

```
tk.Button(self, command=partial(self.set_color, "fg"), ...)
```

The preceding statement performs the same action as the following statement:

```
tk.Button(self, command=lambda: self.set_color("fg"), ...)
```

We did this in order to reuse our `set_color()` method at the same time we introduce the `functools` module. These techniques are very useful in more complex scenarios, especially when you want to compose multiple functions and it is very clear that some arguments are already predefined.

A minor detail to keep in mind is that we shorthanded `foreground` and `background` with `fg` and `bg`, respectively. These strings are unpacked with `**` when configuring the widget in this statement:

```
def set_color(self, option):
    color = askcolor()[1]
    print("Chosen color:", color)
    self.label.config(**{option: color}) # same as (fg=color)
                    or (bg=color)
```

askcolor returns a tuple with two items that represent the selected color—the first one is a tuple of integers that represent the RGB values, and the second one is the hexadecimal code as a string. Since the first representation cannot be directly passed to the widget options, we used the hexadecimal format.

There's more...

In case you want to translate a color name to the RGB format, you can use the winfo_rgb() method on a previously created widget. Since it returns a tuple of integers from 0 to 65535 to represent a 16-bit RGB value, you can convert it to the more common *#RRGGBB* hexadecimal representation by shifting 8 bits to the right:

```
rgb = widget.winfo_rgb("lightblue")
red, green, blue = [x>>8 for x in rgb]
print("#{:02x}{:02x}{:02x}".format(red, green, blue))
```

In the preceding code, we used {:02x} to format each integer into two hexadecimal numbers.

Setting widget fonts

In Tkinter, it is possible to customize the font used in widgets that display text to the users, such as buttons, labels, and entries. By default, the font is system-specific, but you can change it using the font option.

Getting ready

The following application allows users to dynamically change the font family and size of a label with static text. Try around different values to see the results of the font configuration:

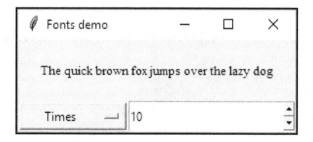

How to do it...

We will have two widgets to modify the font configuration: a drop-down option with font family names and a spinbox to enter the font size:

```python
import tkinter as tk

class App(tk.Tk):
    def __init__(self):
        super().__init__()
        self.title("Fonts demo")
        text = "The quick brown fox jumps over the lazy dog"
        self.label = tk.Label(self, text=text)

        self.family = tk.StringVar()
        self.family.trace("w", self.set_font)
        families = ("Times", "Courier", "Helvetica")
        self.option = tk.OptionMenu(self, self.family, *families)

        self.size = tk.StringVar()
        self.size.trace("w", self.set_font)
        self.spinbox = tk.Spinbox(self, from_=8, to=18,
                                  textvariable=self.size)

        self.family.set(families[0])
        self.size.set("10")
        self.label.pack(padx=20, pady=20)
        self.option.pack(side=tk.LEFT, fill=tk.BOTH, expand=True)
        self.spinbox.pack(side=tk.LEFT, fill=tk.BOTH, expand=True)

    def set_font(self, *args):
        family = self.family.get()
        size = self.size.get()
        self.label.config(font=(family, size))

if __name__ == "__main__":
    app = App()
    app.mainloop()
```

Note that we have set some default values for the Tkinter variables connected to each input.

How it works...

The `FAMILIES` tuple contains the three font families that `Tk` guarantees to support on all platforms: `Times` (Times New Roman), `Courier`, and `Helvetica`. They can be switched with the `OptionMenu` widget, which is connected to the `self.family` variable.

A similar approach is followed to set the font size with `Spinbox`. Both variables trigger the method that changes the `font` label:

```
def set_font(self, *args):
    family = self.family.get()
    size = self.size.get()
    self.label.config(font=(family, size))
```

The tuple passed to the `font` option can also define one or more of the following font styles: bold, roman, italic, underline, and strikethrough:

```
widget1.config(font=("Times", "20", "bold"))
widget2.config(font=("Helvetica", "16", "italic underline"))
```

You can retrieve the complete list of available font families for your platform with the `families()` method from the `tkinter.font` module. Since you need to instantiate the `root` window first, you can use the following script:

```
import tkinter as tk
from tkinter import font

root = tk.Tk()
print(font.families())
```

Tkinter will not throw any error if you use a font family that is not included in the list of available families, but will try to match a similar font.

There's more...

The `tkinter.font` module includes a `Font` class, which can be reused over multiple widgets. The main advantage of modifying a `font` instance is that it affects all the widgets that share it with the `font` option.

Working with the `Font` class is very similar to using font descriptors. For example, this snippet creates a 18-pixel `Courier` bold font:

```
from tkinter import font
courier_18 = font.Font(family="Courier", size=18, weight=font.BOLD)
```

To retrieve or change an option value, you can use the `cget` and `configure` methods as usual:

```
family = courier_18.cget("family")
courier_18.configure(underline=1)
```

See also

- The *Using the options database* recipe

Using the options database

Tkinter defines a concept called *options database*, a mechanism used to customize the appearance of the application without having to specify it for each widget. It allows you to decouple some widget options from the individual widget configuration, providing standardized defaults based on the widget hierarchy.

Getting ready

In this recipe, we will build an application with several widgets that have different styling, which will be defined in the options database:

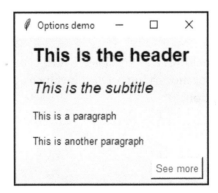

How to do it...

In our example, we will add some options to the database through the option_add() method, which is accessible from all widget classes:

```python
import tkinter as tk

class App(tk.Tk):
    def __init__(self):
        super().__init__()
        self.title("Options demo")
        self.option_add("*font", "helvetica 10")
        self.option_add("*header.font", "helvetica 18 bold")
        self.option_add("*subtitle.font", "helvetica 14 italic")
        self.option_add("*Button.foreground", "blue")
        self.option_add("*Button.background", "white")
        self.option_add("*Button.activeBackground", "gray")
        self.option_add("*Button.activeForeground", "black")

        self.create_label(name="header", text="This is the header")
        self.create_label(name="subtitle", text="This is the subtitle")
        self.create_label(text="This is a paragraph")
        self.create_label(text="This is another paragraph")
        self.create_button(text="See more")

    def create_label(self, **options):
        tk.Label(self, **options).pack(padx=20, pady=5, anchor=tk.W)

    def create_button(self, **options):
        tk.Button(self, **options).pack(padx=5, pady=5, anchor=tk.E)

if __name__ == "__main__":
    app = App()
    app.mainloop()
```

As a result, instead of configuring the font, foreground and background with the rest of the options, Tkinter will use the default values defined in the options database.

How it works...

Let's start by explaining each call to option_add. The first invocation adds an option that sets the font attribute to all the widgets—the wildcard represents any application name:

```python
self.option_add("*font", "helvetica 10")
```

The next call restricts the match to an element with the `header` name—the more specific a rule is, the highest precedence it has. This name is later specified when instantiating the label with `name="header"`:

```
self.option_add("*header.font", "helvetica 18 bold")
```

The same applies to `self.option_add("*subtitle.font", "helvetica 14 italic")`, so each option matches to a different named widget instance.

The next options use the `Button` class name instead of an instance name. This way, you can refer to all widgets of a given class to provide some common defaults:

```
self.option_add("*Button.foreground", "blue")
self.option_add("*Button.background", "white")
self.option_add("*Button.activeBackground", "gray")
self.option_add("*Button.activeForeground", "black")
```

As we have mentioned earlier, the options database uses the widget hierarchy to determine the options that apply to each instance, so if we have nested containers, they can also be used to restrict the options that take precedence.

These configuration options are not applied to existing widgets, only to the ones created after modifying the options database. Therefore, we always recommend calling `option_add()` at the beginning of your applications.

These are some examples where each one is more specific than the preceding one:

- `*Frame*background`: Matches the background of all the widgets within a frame
- `*Frame.background`: Matches the background of all the frames
- `*Frame.myButton.background`: Matches the background of the widget named `myButton`
- `*myFrame.myButton.background`: Matches the background of the widget named `myButton` inside the container named `myFrame`

There's more...

Instead of adding the options programmatically, it is also possible to define them in a separate text file using the following format:

```
*font: helvetica 10
*header.font: helvetica 18 bold
*subtitle.font: helvetica 14 italic
*Button.foreground: blue
*Button.background: white
*Button.activeBackground: gray
*Button.activeForeground: black
```

This file should be loaded into the application using the `option_readfile()` method, and replaces all the calls to `option_add()`. In our example, let's suppose the file is called `my_options_file` and it is placed in the same directory as our script:

```
def __init__(self):
        super().__init__()
        self.title("Options demo")
        self.option_readfile("my_options_file")
        # ...
```

If the file does not exist or its format is invalid, Tkinter will raise `TclError`.

See also

- The *Working with colors* recipe
- The *Setting widget fonts* recipe

Changing the cursor icon

Tkinter allows you to customize the cursor icon while hovering over a widget. This behavior is sometimes enabled by default, like the Entry widget that displays an I-beam pointer.

Getting ready

The following application shows how to display a busy cursor while it is performing a long-running operation, and a cursor with a question mark, typically used in help menus:

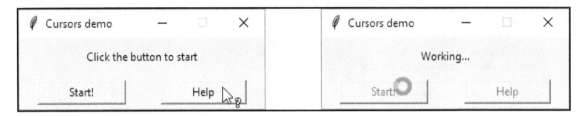

How to do it...

The mouse pointer icon can be changed using the cursor option. In our example, we used the watch value to display the native busy cursor and question_arrow to display the regular arrow with a question mark:

```python
import tkinter as tk

class App(tk.Tk):
    def __init__(self):
        super().__init__()
        self.title("Cursors demo")
        self.resizable(0, 0)
        self.label = tk.Label(self, text="Click the button to start")
        self.btn_launch = tk.Button(self, text="Start!",
                                     command=self.perform_action)
        self.btn_help = tk.Button(self, text="Help",
                                   cursor="question_arrow")

        btn_opts = {"side": tk.LEFT, "expand":True, "fill": tk.X,
                    "ipadx": 30, "padx": 20, "pady": 5}
        self.label.pack(pady=10)
        self.btn_launch.pack(**btn_opts)
        self.btn_help.pack(**btn_opts)

    def perform_action(self):
        self.config(cursor="watch")
        self.btn_launch.config(state=tk.DISABLED)
        self.btn_help.config(state=tk.DISABLED)
        self.label.config(text="Working...")
        self.after(3000, self.end_action)
```

```
    def end_action(self):
        self.config(cursor="arrow")
        self.btn_launch.config(state=tk.NORMAL)
        self.btn_help.config(state=tk.NORMAL)
        self.label.config(text="Done!")

if __name__ == "__main__":
    app = App()
    app.mainloop()
```

You can check out a complete list of valid `cursor` values and the system-specific ones in the official Tcl/Tk documentation at `https://www.tcl.tk/man/tcl/TkCmd/cursors.htm`.

How it works...

If a widget does not specify the `cursor` option, it takes the value defined in the parent container. Therefore, we can easily apply it to all widgets by setting it at the `root` window level. This is done by invoking `set_watch_cursor()` within the `perform_action()` method:

```
def perform_action(self):
    self.config(cursor="watch")
    # ...
```

The exception here is the `Help` button, which explicitly sets the cursor to `question_arrow`. This option can be directly set while instantiating the widget as well:

```
self.btn_help = tk.Button(self, text="Help",
                          cursor="question_arrow")
```

There's more...

Note that if you click on the `Start!` button and place the mouse over the `Help` button before the scheduled method is invoked, the cursor will display as `help` instead of `watch`. This happens because if the `cursor` option of a widget is set, it takes precedence over the `cursor` defined in the parent container.

To avoid this, we can save the current `cursor` value and change it to `watch`, and restore it later. The function that performs this operation can be called recursively in the child widget by iterating over the `winfo_children()` list:

```python
def perform_action(self):
    self.set_watch_cursor(self)
    # ...

def end_action(self):
    self.restore_cursor(self)
    # ...

def set_watch_cursor(self, widget):
    widget._old_cursor = widget.cget("cursor")
    widget.config(cursor="watch")
    for w in widget.winfo_children():
        self.set_watch_cursor(w)

def restore_cursor(self, widget):
    widget.config(cursor=widget._old_cursor)
    for w in widget.winfo_children():
        self.restore_cursor(w)
```

In the preceding code, we added the `_old_cursor` property to each widget, so if you follow a similar approach, keep in mind that you cannot call `restore_cursor()` before `set_watch_cursor()`.

Introducing the Text widget

The Text widget offers an advanced functionality compared with other widget classes. It displays multiple lines of editable text that can be indexed by lines and columns. Additionally, you can refer to ranges of text using tags, which may define a customized appearance and behavior.

Getting ready

The following application shows basic use of the Text widget, where you can dynamically insert and remove text and retrieve the selected content:

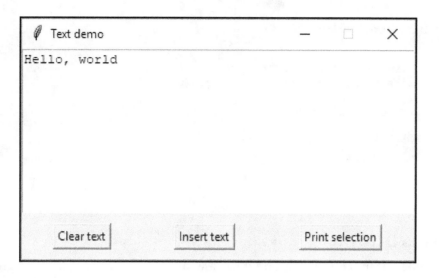

How to do it...

Apart from the `Text` widget, our application contains three buttons that call the methods to clear the whole text content, insert the `"Hello, world"` string in the current cursor position, and print the current selection made with the mouse or the keyboard:

```
import tkinter as tk

class App(tk.Tk):
    def __init__(self):
        super().__init__()
        self.title("Text demo")
        self.resizable(0, 0)
        self.text = tk.Text(self, width=50, height=10)
        self.btn_clear = tk.Button(self, text="Clear text",
                                command=self.clear_text)
        self.btn_insert = tk.Button(self, text="Insert text",
                                command=self.insert_text)
        self.btn_print = tk.Button(self, text="Print selection",
                                command=self.print_selection)
        self.text.pack()
        self.btn_clear.pack(side=tk.LEFT, expand=True, pady=10)
        self.btn_insert.pack(side=tk.LEFT, expand=True, pady=10)
        self.btn_print.pack(side=tk.LEFT, expand=True, pady=10)

    def clear_text(self):
        self.text.delete("1.0", tk.END)
```

```
        def insert_text(self):
            self.text.insert(tk.INSERT, "Hello, world")

        def print_selection(self):
            selection = self.text.tag_ranges(tk.SEL)
            if selection:
                content = self.text.get(*selection)
                print(content)

if __name__ == "__main__":
    app = App()
    app.mainloop()
```

How it works...

Our `Text` widget is initially empty, and it has a width of 50 characters and a height of 10 lines. Apart from allowing users to enter any type of text, we will dive into the methods used by each button to have a better understanding of how to interact with this widget.

The `delete(start, end)` method removes the content from the `start` index to the `end` index. If the second parameter is omitted, it only deletes the character at the `start` position.

In our example, we delete all the text by calling this method from the `1.0` index (column 0 of the first line) to the `tk.END` index, which refers to the last character:

```
    def clear_text(self):
        self.text.delete("1.0", tk.END)
```

The `insert(index, text)` method inserts the given text at the `index` position. Here, we call it with the `INSERT` index, which corresponds to the position of the insertion cursor:

```
    def insert_text(self):
        self.text.insert(tk.INSERT, "Hello, world")
```

The `tag_ranges(tag)` method returns a tuple with the first and last indices of all the ranges with a given `tag`. We used the special `tk.SEL` tag to refer to the current selection. If there is no selection, this call would return an empty tuple. This is combined with the `get(start, end)` method, which returns the text in a given range:

```
    def print_selection(self):
        selection = self.text.tag_ranges(tk.SEL)
        if selection:
            content = self.text.get(*selection)
            print(content)
```

Since the SEL tag corresponds to only one range, we can safely unpack it to call the get method.

Adding tags to the Text widget

In this recipe, you will learn how to configure the behavior of a tagged range of characters within a Text widget.

All the concepts are the same as those that apply to regular widgets, such as event sequences or configuration options, which have already been covered in previous recipes. The main difference is that we need to work with the text indices to identify the tagged content, instead of using object references.

Getting ready

To illustrate how to use the text tags, we will create a Text widget that simulates the insertion of hyperlinks. When clicked, this link will open the selected URL with the default browser.

For instance, if the user enters the following content, the **python.org** text can be tagged as a hyperlink:

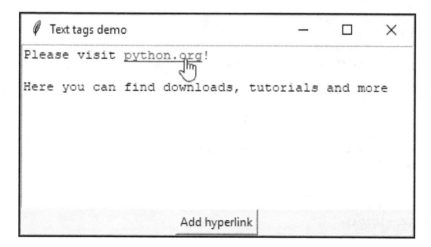

How to do it...

For this application, we will define a tag named `"link"`, which represents a clickable hyperlink. This tag will be added to the current selection using a button, and the mouse click will trigger the event to open the link in a browser:

```python
import tkinter as tk
import webbrowser

class App(tk.Tk):
    def __init__(self):
        super().__init__()
        self.title("Text tags demo")
        self.text = tk.Text(self, width=50, height=10)
        self.btn_link = tk.Button(self, text="Add hyperlink",
                                  command=self.add_hyperlink)

        self.text.tag_config("link", foreground="blue", underline=1)
        self.text.tag_bind("link", "<Button-1>", self.open_link)
        self.text.tag_bind("link", "<Enter>",
                           lambda _: self.text.config(cursor="hand2"))
        self.text.tag_bind("link", "<Leave>",
                           lambda e: self.text.config(cursor=""))

        self.text.pack()
        self.btn_link.pack(expand=True)

    def add_hyperlink(self):
        selection = self.text.tag_ranges(tk.SEL)
        if selection:
            self.text.tag_add("link", *selection)

    def open_link(self, event):
        position = "@{},{} + 1c".format(event.x, event.y)
        index = self.text.index(position)
        prevrange = self.text.tag_prevrange("link", index)
        url = self.text.get(*prevrange)
        webbrowser.open(url)

if __name__ == "__main__":
    app = App()
    app.mainloop()
```

How it works...

First, we will initialize the tag by configuring the color and underline style. We add event bindings to open the clicked text with a browser and to change the cursor appearance while placing the mouse over the tagged text:

```
def __init__(self):
    # ...
    self.text.tag_config("link", foreground="blue", underline=1)
    self.text.tag_bind("link", "<Button-1>", self.open_link)
    self.text.tag_bind("link", "<Enter>",
                    lambda e: self.text.config(cursor="hand2"))
    self.text.tag_bind("link", "<Leave>",
                    lambda e: self.text.config(cursor=""))
```

Within the `open_link` method, we transform the clicked position to the corresponding line and column using the `index` method of the `Text` class:

```
position = "@{},{} + 1c".format(event.x, event.y)
index = self.text.index(position)
prevrange = self.text.tag_prevrange("link", index)
```

Note that the position corresponding to the clicked index is `"@x,y"`, but we moved it to the next character. We do this because `tag_prevrange` returns the preceding range to the given index, so it will not return the current range if we click on the first character.

Finally, we will retrieve the text from the range and open it with the default browser using the `open` function from the `webbrowser` module:

```
url = self.text.get(*prevrange)
webbrowser.open(url)
```

There's more...

Since the `webbrowser.open` function does not check whether the URL is valid, this application can be improved by including a basic hyperlink validation. For instance, you can use the `urlparse` function to verify that the URL has a network location:

```
from urllib.parse import urlparse

def validate_hyperlink(self, url):
    return urlparse(url).netloc
```

Although this solution is not intended to handle some corner cases, it might serve as a first approach to discarding most invalid URLs.

In general, you can use tags to create complex text-based programs, such as an IDE with syntax highlighting. In fact, IDLE—bundled in the default Python implementation—is based on Tkinter.

See also

- The *Changing the cursor icon* recipe
- The *Introducing the Text widget* recipe

Dialogs and Menus

4

In this chapter, we will cover the following recipes:

- Showing alert dialogs
- Asking for user confirmation
- Choosing files and directories
- Saving data into a file
- Creating a menu bar
- Using variables in menus
- Displaying context menus
- Opening a secondary window
- Passing variables between windows
- Handling window deletion

Introduction

Almost every nontrivial GUI application is composed of multiple views. In browsers, this is achieved by navigating from one HTML page to another, and in desktop applications, it is represented by multiple windows and dialogs that users can interact with.

So far, we have learned how to create only a root window, which is associated with the Tcl interpreter. However, Tkinter allows us to create multiple top-level windows under the same application, and it also includes specific modules with built-in dialogs.

Another way to structure how to navigate in your application is using menus, which are usually displayed under the title bar in desktop applications. In Tkinter, these menus are represented by a widget class; we will dive later into its methods and how to integrate it with the rest of our application.

Showing alert dialogs

A common use case for dialogs is notifying users of events that occurred in our application, such as that a record has been saved, or that it failed to open a file. We will now take a look at some of the basic functions included in Tkinter to display informational dialogs.

Getting ready

Our program will have three buttons, where each one illustrates a different dialog with a static title and message. This type of dialog boxes have only a button to confirm and close the dialog:

When you run the preceding example, note that each dialog plays the corresponding sound defined by your platform, and the button label is translated to your language:

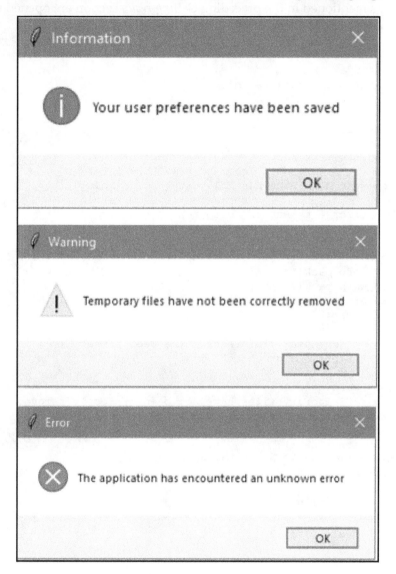

How to do it...

The three dialogs mentioned in the preceding *Getting ready* section are opened with the showinfo, showwarning, and showerror functions from the tkinter.messagebox module:

```python
import tkinter as tk
import tkinter.messagebox as mb

class App(tk.Tk):
    def __init__(self):
        super().__init__()
        btn_info = tk.Button(self, text="Show Info",
                             command=self.show_info)
        btn_warn = tk.Button(self, text="Show Warning",
                             command=self.show_warning)
        btn_error = tk.Button(self, text="Show Error",
                              command=self.show_error)

        opts = {'padx': 40, 'pady': 5, 'expand': True, 'fill': tk.BOTH}
        btn_info.pack(**opts)
        btn_warn.pack(**opts)
        btn_error.pack(**opts)

    def show_info(self):
        msg = "Your user preferences have been saved"
        mb.showinfo("Information", msg)

    def show_warning(self):
        msg = "Temporary files have not been correctly removed"
        mb.showwarning("Warning", msg)

    def show_error(self):
        msg = "The application has encountered an unknown error"
        mb.showerror("Error", msg)

if __name__ == "__main__":
    app = App()
    app.mainloop()
```

How it works...

First, we imported the `tkinter.messagebox` module with the shorter alias `mb`. This module was named `tkMessageBox` in Python 2, so this syntax also helps us to isolate compatibility issues in a single statement.

Each dialog is commonly used depending on the type of information that is notified to the users:

- `showinfo`: The operation completed successfully
- `showwarning`: The operation completed but something did not behave as expected
- `showerror`: The operation failed due to an error

These three functions receive two strings as input arguments: the first one is displayed on the title bar, and the second one corresponds to the message shown by the dialog.

Dialog messages can also spawn across multiple lines by adding the new line character, `\n`.

Asking for user confirmation

Other types of dialogs included in Tkinter are those used to ask for user confirmation, such as the ones shown when we want to save a file and are about to override an existing one with the same name.

These dialogs differ from the preceding one because the values returned by the functions will depend on the confirmation button clicked by the user. This way, we can interact with the program to indicate whether to continue or cancel the action.

Getting ready

In this recipe, we will cover the remaining dialog functions defined in the `tkinter.messagebox` module. Each button is labeled with the type of dialog that is opened when clicked:

Since there are a few differences among these dialogs, you can try them out to see which one may better fit your needs for each situation:

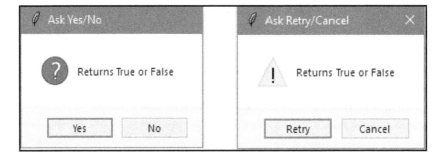

How to do it...

As we did in our preceding example, we will import `tkinter.messagebox` with the `import ... as` syntax and call each function with `title` and `message`:

```
import tkinter as tk
import tkinter.messagebox as mb
```

```
class App(tk.Tk):
    def __init__(self):
        super().__init__()
        self.create_button(mb.askyesno, "Ask Yes/No",
                           "Returns True or False")
        self.create_button(mb.askquestion, "Ask a question",
                           "Returns 'yes' or 'no'")
        self.create_button(mb.askokcancel, "Ask Ok/Cancel",
                           "Returns True or False")
        self.create_button(mb.askretrycancel, "Ask Retry/Cancel",
                           "Returns True or False")
        self.create_button(mb.askyesnocancel, "Ask Yes/No/Cancel",
                           "Returns True, False or None")

    def create_button(self, dialog, title, message):
        command = lambda: print(dialog(title, message))
        btn = tk.Button(self, text=title, command=command)
        btn.pack(padx=40, pady=5, expand=True, fill=tk.BOTH)

if __name__ == "__main__":
    app = App()
    app.mainloop()
```

How it works...

To avoid repeating the code for the button instantiation and the callback method, we defined a `create_button` method to reuse it as many times as we need to add all the buttons with their dialogs. The commands simply print the result of the `dialog` function passed as a parameter so that we can see the values returned, depending on the button clicked, to answer the dialog.

Choosing files and directories

File dialogs allow users to select one or multiple files from the filesystem. In Tkinter, these functions are declared in the `tkinter.filedialog` module, which also includes dialogs for choosing directories. It also lets you customize the behavior of a new dialog, such as filtering the files by their extension or choosing the initial directory displayed by the dialog.

Getting ready

Our application will contain two buttons. The first will be labeled **Choose file**, and it will display a dialog to select a file. By default, it will only show files with the .txt extension:

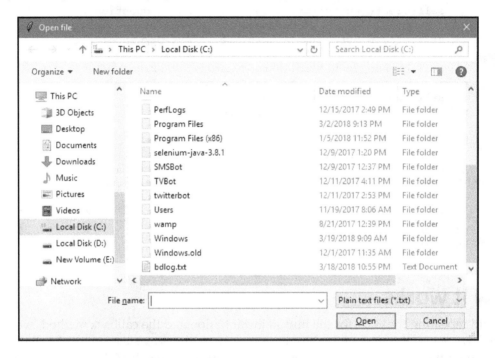

The second button will be **Choose directory**, and it will open a similar dialog to select a directory:

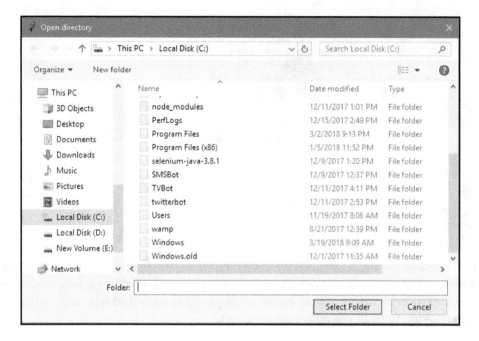

Both buttons will print the full path to the selected file or directory, and will not perform any action if the dialog is canceled.

How to do it...

The first button of our application will trigger a call to the `askopenfilename` function, whereas the second one will call the `askdirectory` function:

```
import tkinter as tk
import tkinter.filedialog as fd

class App(tk.Tk):
    def __init__(self):
        super().__init__()
        btn_file = tk.Button(self, text="Choose file",
                          command=self.choose_file)
        btn_dir = tk.Button(self, text="Choose directory",
                          command=self.choose_directory)
        btn_file.pack(padx=60, pady=10)
        btn_dir.pack(padx=60, pady=10)

    def choose_file(self):
        filetypes = (("Plain text files", "*.txt"),
```

```
                    ("Images", "*.jpg *.gif *.png"),
                    ("All files", "*"))
        filename = fd.askopenfilename(title="Open file",
                    initialdir="/", filetypes=filetypes)
        if filename:
            print(filename)

    def choose_directory(self):
        directory = fd.askdirectory(title="Open directory",
                                    initialdir="/")
        if directory:
            print(directory)

if __name__ == "__main__":
    app = App()
    app.mainloop()
```

Since these dialogs can be dismissed, we added conditional statements to check whether the dialog function returns a non-empty string before printing it into the console. We would need this validation in any application that must perform an action with this path, such as reading or copying files, or changing permissions.

How it works...

We create the first dialog with the `askopenfilename` function, which returns a string that represents the full path to the chosen file. It accepts the following optional arguments:

- `title`: Title displayed in the dialog's title bar.
- `initialdir`: Initial directory.
- `filetypes`: Sequence of tuples of two strings. The first one is a label indicating the type of the file in a human-readable format, whereas the second one is a pattern to match the filename.
- `multiple`: Boolean value to indicate whether users may select multiple files.
- `defaultextension`: Extension added to the filename if it is not explicitly given.

In our example, we set the initial directory to the root folder and a custom title. In our tuple of file types, we have the following three valid choices: text files saved with the `.txt` extension; images with the `.jpg`, `.gif`, and `.png` extensions; and the wildcard (`"*"`) to match all files.

Note that these patterns do not necessarily match the format of the data contained in the file since it is possible to rename a file with a different extension:

```
filetypes = (("Plain text files", "*.txt"),
             ("Images", "*.jpg *.gif *.png"),
             ("All files", "*"))
filename = fd.askopenfilename(title="Open file", initialdir="/",
                             filetypes=filetypes)
```

The `askdirectory` function also takes the `title` and `initialdir` parameters, and a `mustexist` Boolean option to indicate whether users have to pick an existing directory:

```
directory = fd.askdirectory(title="Open directory", initialdir="/")
```

There's more...

The `tkinter.filedialog` module includes some variations of these functions that allow you to directly retrieve the file objects.

For instance, `askopenfile` returns the file object corresponding to the selected file, instead of having to call `open` with the path returned by `askopenfilename`. We still have to check whether the dialog has not been dismissed before calling the file methods:

```
import tkinter.filedialog as fd

filetypes = (("Plain text files", "*.txt"),)
my_file = fd.askopenfile(title="Open file", filetypes=filetypes)
if my_file:
    print(my_file.readlines())
    my_file.close()
```

Saving data into a file

Apart from selecting existing files and directories, it is also possible to create a new file using Tkinter dialogs. They can be used to persist data generated by our application, letting users choose the name and location of the new file.

Getting ready

We will use the **Save file** dialog to write the contents of a Text widget into a plain text file:

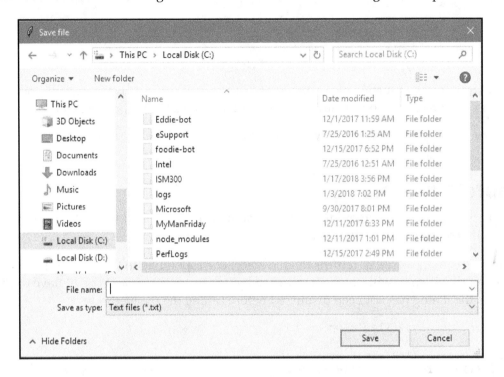

How to do it...

To open a dialog to save a file, we call the `asksaveasfile` function from the `tkinter.filedialog` module. It internally creates a file object with the `'w'` mode for writing, or None if the dialog is dismissed:

```python
import tkinter as tk
import tkinter.filedialog as fd

class App(tk.Tk):
    def __init__(self):
        super().__init__()
        self.text = tk.Text(self, height=10, width=50)
        self.btn_save = tk.Button(self, text="Save",
                                  command=self.save_file)
```

```
        self.text.pack()
        self.btn_save.pack(pady=10, ipadx=5)

    def save_file(self):
        contents = self.text.get(1.0, tk.END)
        new_file = fd.asksaveasfile(title="Save file",
                                    defaultextension=".txt",
                                    filetypes=(("Text files",
                                               "*.txt"),))
        if new_file:
            new_file.write(contents)
            new_file.close()

if __name__ == "__main__":
    app = App()
    app.mainloop()
```

How it works...

The `asksaveasfile` function accepts the same optional parameters as the `askopenfile` function, but also allows you to add the file extension by default with the `defaultextension` option.

To prevent users from accidentally overriding previous files, this dialog automatically warns you if you try to save a new file with the same name as an existing one.

With the file object, we can write the contents of the Text widget—always remember to close the file to free the resources taken by the object:

```
contents = self.text.get(1.0, tk.END)
new_file.write(contents)
new_file.close()
```

There's more...

In the preceding recipe, we saw that there is a function equivalent to `askopenfilename` that returns a file object instead of a string, named `askopenfile`.

To save files, there is also a `asksaveasfilename` function that returns the path of the selected file. You can use this function if you want to modify the path or perform any validation before opening the file for writing.

See also

- The *Choosing files and directories* recipe

Creating a menu bar

Complex GUIs typically use menu bars to organize the actions and navigations that are available in our application. This pattern is also used to group operations that are closely related, such as the **File** menu included in most text editors.

Tkinter natively supports these menus, which are displayed with the look and feel of the target desktop environment. Therefore, you do not have to simulate them with frames or labels, because you would lose the cross-platform features that have already been built into Tkinter.

Getting ready

We will start by adding a menu bar to a root window with a nested drop-down menu. On Windows 10, this is displayed as follows:

How to do it...

Tkinter has a Menu widget class that can be used for many kinds of menus, including top menu bars. As any other widget classes, menus are instantiated with the parent container as the first argument and some optional configuration options:

```
import tkinter as tk

class App(tk.Tk):
    def __init__(self):
        super().__init__()
        menu = tk.Menu(self)
        file_menu = tk.Menu(menu, tearoff=0)

        file_menu.add_command(label="New file")
        file_menu.add_command(label="Open")
        file_menu.add_separator()
        file_menu.add_command(label="Save")
        file_menu.add_command(label="Save as...")

        menu.add_cascade(label="File", menu=file_menu)
        menu.add_command(label="About")
        menu.add_command(label="Quit", command=self.destroy)
        self.config(menu=menu)

if __name__ == "__main__":
    app = App()
    app.mainloop()
```

If you run the preceding script, you can see that the File entry shows the secondary menu, and you can close the application by clicking the Quit menu button.

How it works...

First, we instantiate each menu, indicating the parent container. The tearoff option, set to 1 by default, indicates that the menu can be detached by clicking on the dashed line of its top border. This behavior is not applied to the top menu bar, but if we want to deactivate this functionality, we have to set this option to 0:

```
    def __init__(self):
        super().__init__()
        menu = tk.Menu(self)
        file_menu = tk.Menu(menu, tearoff=0)
```

Menu entries are arranged in the same order that they are added, using the `add_command`, `add_separator`, and `add_cascade` methods:

```
menu.add_cascade(label="File", menu=file_menu)
menu.add_command(label="About")
menu.add_command(label="Quit", command=self.destroy)
```

Usually, `add_command` is called with a `command` option, which is the callback invoked when the entry is clicked. There are no arguments passed to the callback function, exactly as with the `command` option of the Button widget.

For illustration purposes, we only added this option to the `Quit` entry to destroy the `Tk` instance and close the application.

Finally, we attach the menu to the top-level window by calling `self.config(menu=menu)`. Note that each top-level window can only have a single menu bar configured.

Using variables in menus

Apart from calling commands and nesting submenus, it is also possible to connect Tkinter variables to menu entries.

Getting ready

We will add a check button entry and three radio button entries to the **Options** submenu, divided by a separator. There will be two underlying Tkinter variables to store the selected values, so we can retrieve them easily from other methods of our application:

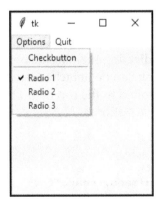

How to do it...

These types of entries are added with the `add_checkbutton` and `add_radiobutton` methods of the `Menu` widget class. Like with regular radio buttons, all are connected to the same Tkinter variable, but each one sets a different value:

```python
import tkinter as tk

class App(tk.Tk):
    def __init__(self):
        super().__init__()
        self.checked = tk.BooleanVar()
        self.checked.trace("w", self.mark_checked)
        self.radio = tk.StringVar()
        self.radio.set("1")
        self.radio.trace("w", self.mark_radio)
        menu = tk.Menu(self)
        submenu = tk.Menu(menu, tearoff=0)

        submenu.add_checkbutton(label="Checkbutton", onvalue=True,
                                offvalue=False, variable=self.checked)
        submenu.add_separator()
        submenu.add_radiobutton(label="Radio 1", value="1",
                                variable=self.radio)
        submenu.add_radiobutton(label="Radio 2", value="2",
                                variable=self.radio)
        submenu.add_radiobutton(label="Radio 3", value="3",
                                variable=self.radio)

        menu.add_cascade(label="Options", menu=submenu)
        menu.add_command(label="Quit", command=self.destroy)
        self.config(menu=menu)

    def mark_checked(self, *args):
        print(self.checked.get())

    def mark_radio(self, *args):
        print(self.radio.get())

if __name__ == "__main__":
    app = App()
    app.mainloop()
```

Additionally, we are tracing the variable changes so you can see the values printed on the console when you run this application.

How it works...

To connect a Boolean variable to the `Checkbutton` entry, we first define `BooleanVar` and then create the entry by calling `add_checkbutton` using the `variable` option.

Remember that the `onvalue` and `offvalue` options should match the type of the Tkinter variable, as we do with regular RadioButton and CheckButton widgets:

```
self.checked = tk.BooleanVar()
self.checked.trace("w", self.mark_checked)
# ...
submenu.add_checkbutton(label="Checkbutton", onvalue=True,
                        offvalue=False, variable=self.checked)
```

`Radiobutton` entries are created in a similar fashion using the `add_radiobutton` method, and only a single `value` option to set to the Tkinter variable when the radio is clicked. Since `StringVar` initially holds the empty string value, we set it to the first radio value so that it will display as checked:

```
self.radio = tk.StringVar()
self.radio.set("1")
self.radio.trace("w", self.mark_radio)
# ...
submenu.add_radiobutton(label="Radio 1", value="1",
                        variable=self.radio)
submenu.add_radiobutton(label="Radio 2", value="2",
                        variable=self.radio)
submenu.add_radiobutton(label="Radio 3", value="3",
                        variable=self.radio)
```

Both variables trace the changes with the `mark_checked` and `mark_radio` methods, which simply print the variable values into the console.

Displaying context menus

Tkinter menus do not necessarily have to be located on the menu bar, but they can actually be freely placed at any coordinate. These types of menus are called context menus, and they are usually displayed when users right-click on an item.

Context menus are widely used in GUI applications; for instance, file browsers display them to offer the available operations over the selected file, so it is intuitive for users to know how to interact with them.

Getting ready

We will build a context menu for a Text widget to display some common actions of text editors, such as **Cut**, **Copy**, **Paste**, and **Delete**:

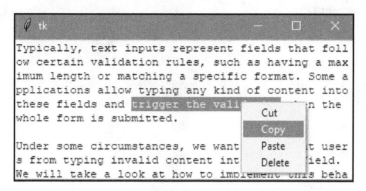

How to do it...

Instead of configuring a menu instance with a top-level container as a top menu bar, you can explicitly place it using its `post` method.

All the commands in the menu entries call a method that uses the text instance to retrieve the current selection or the insertion position:

```python
import tkinter as tk

class App(tk.Tk):
    def __init__(self):
        super().__init__()
        self.menu = tk.Menu(self, tearoff=0)
        self.menu.add_command(label="Cut", command=self.cut_text)
        self.menu.add_command(label="Copy", command=self.copy_text)
        self.menu.add_command(label="Paste", command=self.paste_text)
        self.menu.add_command(label="Delete", command=self.delete_text)

        self.text = tk.Text(self, height=10, width=50)
        self.text.bind("<Button-3>", self.show_popup)
        self.text.pack()

    def show_popup(self, event):
        self.menu.post(event.x_root, event.y_root)

    def cut_text(self):
```

```
        self.copy_text()
        self.delete_text()

    def copy_text(self):
        selection = self.text.tag_ranges(tk.SEL)
        if selection:
            self.clipboard_clear()
            self.clipboard_append(self.text.get(*selection))

    def paste_text(self):
        self.text.insert(tk.INSERT, self.clipboard_get())

    def delete_text(self):
        selection = self.text.tag_ranges(tk.SEL)
        if selection:
            self.text.delete(*selection)

if __name__ == "__main__":
    app = App()
    app.mainloop()
```

How it works...

We bind the right-click event to the `show_popup` handler for the text instance, which displays the menu with its top-left corner over the clicked position. Each time this event is triggered, the same menu instance is displayed again:

```
def show_popup(self, event):
    self.menu.post(event.x_root, event.y_root)
```

The following methods are available for all widget classes to interact with the clipboard:

- `clipboard_clear()`: Clears the data from the clipboard
- `clipboard_append(string)`: Appends a string to the clipboard
- `clipboard_get()`: Returns the data from the clipboard

The callback method for the *copy* action gets the current selection and adds it to the clipboard:

```
def copy_text(self):
    selection = self.text.tag_ranges(tk.SEL)
    if selection:
        self.clipboard_clear()
        self.clipboard_append(self.text.get(*selection))
```

The *paste* action inserts the clipboard contents into the insertion cursor position, defined by the INSERT index. We have to wrap this in a try...except block, since calling clipboard_get raises a TclError if the clipboard is empty:

```
def paste_text(self):
    try:
        self.text.insert(tk.INSERT, self.clipboard_get())
    except tk.TclError:
        pass
```

The *delete* action does not interact with the clipboard, but removes the contents of the current selection:

```
def delete_text(self):
    selection = self.text.tag_ranges(tk.SEL)
    if selection:
        self.text.delete(*selection)
```

Since the cut action is a combination of copy and delete, we reused these methods to compose its callback function.

There's more...

The postcommand option allows you to reconfigure a menu each time it is displayed with the post method. To illustrate how to use this option, we will disable the cut, copy, and delete entries if there is no current selection in the Text widget and disable the paste entry if there are no contents in the clipboard.

Like the rest of our callback functions, we pass a reference to a method of our class to add this configuration option:

```
def __init__(self):
    super().__init__()
    self.menu = tk.Menu(self, tearoff=0,
    postcommand=self.enable_selection)
```

Then, we check whether the SEL range exists to determine whether the state of the entries should be ACTIVE or DISABLED. This value is passed to the entryconfig method, which takes the index of the entry to configure as its first argument, and the list of options to be updated—remember that menu entries are 0 indexed:

```
def enable_selection(self):
    state_selection = tk.ACTIVE if self.text.tag_ranges(tk.SEL)
                      else tk.DISABLED
```

```
state_clipboard = tk.ACTIVE
try:
    self.clipboard_get()
except tk.TclError:
    state_clipboard = tk.DISABLED

self.menu.entryconfig(0, state=state_selection)  # Cut
self.menu.entryconfig(1, state=state_selection)  # Copy
self.menu.entryconfig(2, state=state_clipboard)  # Paste
self.menu.entryconfig(3, state=state_selection)  # Delete
```

For instance, all the entries should be grayed out if there is no selection or if there are no contents on the clipboard:

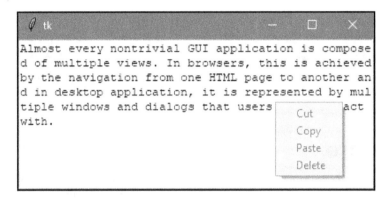

With `entryconfig`, it is also possible to configure many other options, such as the label, font, and background. Refer to `https://www.tcl.tk/man/tcl8.6/TkCmd/menu.htm#M48` for a complete reference of available entry options.

Opening a secondary window

The root `Tk` instance represents the main window of our GUI—when it is destroyed, the application quits and the event mainloop finishes.

However, there is another Tkinter class to create additional top-level windows in our application, called `Toplevel`. You can use this class to display any kind of window, from custom dialogs to wizard forms.

Getting ready

We will start by creating a simple window that is opened when a button of the main window is clicked. It will contain a button that closes it and returns the focus to the main window:

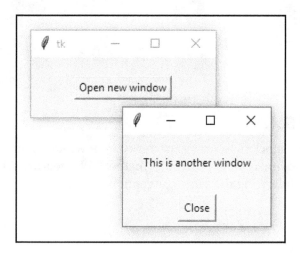

How to do it...

The `Toplevel` widget class creates a new top-level window, which acts as a parent container like the `Tk` instance does. Unlike the `Tk` class, you can instantiate as many top-level windows as you like:

```
import tkinter as tk

class Window(tk.Toplevel):
    def __init__(self, parent):
        super().__init__(parent)
        self.label = tk.Label(self, text="This is another window")
        self.button = tk.Button(self, text="Close",
                                command=self.destroy)

        self.label.pack(padx=20, pady=20)
        self.button.pack(pady=5, ipadx=2, ipady=2)

class App(tk.Tk):
    def __init__(self):
        super().__init__()
```

```
        self.btn = tk.Button(self, text="Open new window",
                                command=self.open_window)
        self.btn.pack(padx=50, pady=20)

    def open_window(self):
        window = Window(self)
        window.grab_set()

if __name__ == "__main__":
    app = App()
    app.mainloop()
```

How it works...

We define a `Toplevel` subclass to represent our custom window, whose relationship with the parent window is defined in its __init__ method. Widgets are added to this window as usual, since we are following the same conventions as when we subclass `Tk`:

```
class Window(tk.Toplevel):
    def __init__(self, parent):
        super().__init__(parent)
```

The window is opened by simply creating a new instance, but in order to make it receive all the events, we have to call its `grab_set` method. This prevents users from interacting with the main window until this one is closed:

```
def open_window(self):
    window = Window(self)
    window.grab_set()
```

Handling window deletion

Under some circumstances, you might want to perform an action before the user closes a top-level window, for instance, to prevent you losing unsaved work. Tkinter allows you to intercept this type of event to conditionally destroy the window.

Getting ready

We will reuse the App class from the preceding recipe, and we will modify the Window class so that it shows a dialog to confirm closing the window:

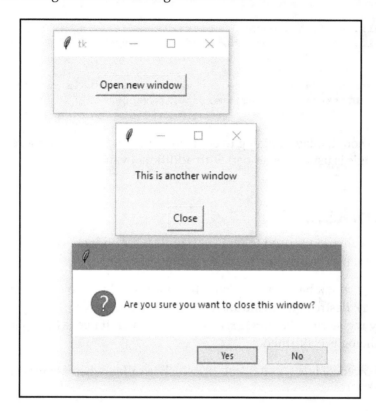

How to do it...

In Tkinter, we can detect when a window is about to be closed by registering a handler function for the WM_DELETE_WINDOW protocol. This can be triggered by clicking on the **X** button of the title bar on most desktop environments:

```
import tkinter as tk
import tkinter.messagebox as mb

class Window(tk.Toplevel):
    def __init__(self, parent):
        super().__init__(parent)
```

```
        self.protocol("WM_DELETE_WINDOW", self.confirm_delete)

        self.label = tk.Label(self, text="This is another window")
        self.button = tk.Button(self, text="Close",
                                command=self.destroy)

        self.label.pack(padx=20, pady=20)
        self.button.pack(pady=5, ipadx=2, ipady=2)

    def confirm_delete(self):
        message = "Are you sure you want to close this window?"
        if mb.askyesno(message=message, parent=self):
            self.destroy()
```

Our handler method displays a dialog to confirm window deletion. In more complex programs, this logic is usually extended with additional validations.

How it works...

While the `bind()` method is used to register handlers for widget events, the `protocol` method does the same for window manager protocols.

The `WM_DELETE_WINDOW` handler is called when a top-level window is about to be closed, and, by default, `Tk` destroys the window for which it was received. Since we are overriding this behavior by registering the `confirm_delete` handler, it needs to explicitly destroy the window if the dialog is confirmed.

Another useful protocol is `WM_TAKE_FOCUS`, which is called when a window takes the focus.

There's more...

Bear in mind that to keep the focus of the second window when the dialog is displayed, we have to pass the reference to the top-level instance, the `parent` option, to the dialog function:

```
    if mb.askyesno(message=message, parent=self):
        self.destroy()
```

Otherwise, the dialog will take the root window as its parent, and you would see that it pops over the second window. These quirks may confuse your users, so it is a good practice to correctly set the parent of each top-level instance or dialog.

Passing variables between windows

Two different windows may need to share information during program execution. While this data might be saved to disk and read from the window that consumes it, in some circumstances it is more straightforward to handle it in memory and simply pass this information as variables.

Getting ready

The main window will contain three radio buttons to select the type of user that we want to create, and the secondary window will open the form to fill in the user data:

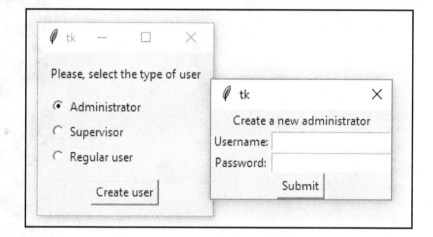

How to do it...

To hold the user data, we create `namedtuple` with fields that represent each user instance. This function from the `collections` module receives the type name and a sequence of field names, and returns a tuple subclass to create lightweight objects with the given fields:

```python
import tkinter as tk
from collections import namedtuple

User = namedtuple("User", ["username", "password", "user_type"])

class UserForm(tk.Toplevel):
    def __init__(self, parent, user_type):
        super().__init__(parent)
```

```
        self.username = tk.StringVar()
        self.password = tk.StringVar()
        self.user_type = user_type

        label = tk.Label(self, text="Create a new " +
                         user_type.lower())
        entry_name = tk.Entry(self, textvariable=self.username)
        entry_pass = tk.Entry(self, textvariable=self.password,
                              show="*")
        btn = tk.Button(self, text="Submit", command=self.destroy)

        label.grid(row=0, columnspan=2)
        tk.Label(self, text="Username:").grid(row=1, column=0)
        tk.Label(self, text="Password:").grid(row=2, column=0)
        entry_name.grid(row=1, column=1)
        entry_pass.grid(row=2, column=1)
        btn.grid(row=3, columnspan=2)

    def open(self):
        self.grab_set()
        self.wait_window()
        username = self.username.get()
        password = self.password.get()
        return User(username, password, self.user_type)


class App(tk.Tk):
    def __init__(self):
        super().__init__()
        user_types = ("Administrator", "Supervisor", "Regular user")
        self.user_type = tk.StringVar()
        self.user_type.set(user_types[0])

        label = tk.Label(self, text="Please, select the type of user")
        radios = [tk.Radiobutton(self, text=t, value=t, \
                  variable=self.user_type) for t in user_types]
        btn = tk.Button(self, text="Create user",
                        command=self.open_window)

        label.pack(padx=10, pady=10)
        for radio in radios:
            radio.pack(padx=10, anchor=tk.W)
        btn.pack(pady=10)

    def open_window(self):
        window = UserForm(self, self.user_type.get())
        user = window.open()
        print(user)
```

```
if __name__ == "__main__":
    app = App()
    app.mainloop()
```

When the execution flow returns to the main window, the user data is printed to the console.

How it works...

Most of the code of this recipe have already been covered in other recipes, and the main difference is contained in the `open()` method of the `UserForm` class, where we moved the call to `grab_set()`. However, the `wait_window()` method is what actually stops the execution and prevents us from returning the data before the form has been modified:

```
def open(self):
    self.grab_set()
    self.wait_window()
    username = self.username.get()
    password = self.password.get()
    return User(username, password, self.user_type)
```

It is important to remark that `wait_window()` enters a local event loop, which finishes when the window is destroyed. Although it is possible to pass the widget we want to wait to be removed, we can omit it to implicitly refer to the instance that calls this method.

When the `UserForm` instance is destroyed, the execution of the `open()` method continues, and it returns the `User` object that can now be used in the `App` class:

```
def open_window(self):
    window = UserForm(self, self.user_type.get())
    user = window.open()
    print(user)
```

5
Object-Oriented Programming and MVC

In this chapter, we will cover the following recipes:

- Structuring our data with a class
- Composing widgets to display information
- Reading records from a CSV file
- Persisting data into a SQLite database
- Refactoring using the MVC pattern

Introduction

So far, all our applications held data in memory as local variables or attributes. However, we also want to be able to persist information so that it is not lost when the program is closed.

In this chapter, we will discuss how to represent and display this data using **object-oriented programming** (**OOP**) principles and applying the **Model-View-Controller** (**MVC**) pattern. In short, this pattern proposes three components into which we can divide our GUI: a **model** that holds the application data, a **view** that displays this data, and a **controller** that handles user events and connects the view with the model.

These concepts are related to how we manipulate and persist information, and in turn help us to improve the organization of our programs. Most of these recipes are not specific to Tkinter, and you can apply the same principles to other GUI libraries.

Structuring our data with a class

We will take the example of a contact list application to illustrate how to model our data using Python classes. Even though the user interface may offer lots of different functionalities, we will need to define what attributes represent our domain model—in our case, each individual contact.

Getting ready

Every contact will contain the following information:

- A first and last name, which must not be empty
- An email address, such as `john.doe@acme.com`
- A phone number with the *(123) 4567890* format

With this abstraction, we can start writing the code of our `Contact` class.

How to do it...

First, we define a couple of utility functions that we will reuse to validate the fields that are mandatory or must follow a specific format:

```
def required(value, message):
    if not value:
        raise ValueError(message)
    return value

def matches(value, regex, message):
    if value and not regex.match(value):
        raise ValueError(message)
    return value
```

Then, we define our `Contact` class and its __init__ method. We set here all the parameters to the corresponding fields. We also store the compiled regular expressions as class attributes since we will use them for every instance to perform the field validations:

```
import re

class Contact(object):
    email_regex = re.compile(r"[^@]+@[^@]+\.[^@]+")
    phone_regex = re.compile(r"\([0-9]{3}\)\s[0-9]{7}")
```

```
def __init__(self, last_name, first_name, email, phone):
    self.last_name = last_name
    self.first_name = first_name
    self.email = email
    self.phone = phone
```

However, this definition is not enough to enforce the validations for each field. To do so, we use the `@property` decorator, which allow us to wrap access to an internal attribute:

```
@property
def last_name(self):
    return self._last_name

@last_name.setter
def last_name(self, value):
    self._last_name = required(value, "Last name is required")
```

The same technique is applied for `first_name` since it is also mandatory. The `email` and `phone` attributes follow a similar approach, using the `matches` function with the corresponding regular expression:

```
@property
def email(self):
    return self._email

@email.setter
def email(self, value):
    self._email = matches(value, self.email_regex,
                          "Invalid email format")
```

This script should be saved as `chapter5_01.py`, since we will import it later in future recipes with this name.

How it works...

As we mentioned earlier, the `property` descriptor is a mechanism for triggering function calls while accessing the attributes of an object.

In our example, they wrap access to the internal attributes with a leading underscore, like so:

```
contact.first_name = "John"  # Stores "John" in contact._first_name
print(contact.first_name)    # Reads "John" from contact._first_name
contact.last_name = ""       # ValueError raised by the required function
```

The `property` descriptor is typically used with the `@decorated` syntax—remember to always use the same name for the decorated functions:

```
@property
def last_name(self):
    # ...

@last_name.setter
def last_name(self, value):
    # ...
```

There's more...

You may find the complete implementation of our `Contact` class quite verbose and repetitive. For each attribute, we will need to assign it in the `__init__` method and write its corresponding getter and setter methods.

Fortunately, we have several alternatives to reduce this amount of boilerplate code. The `namedtuple` function from the standard library allows us to create lightweight tuple subclasses with named fields:

```
from collections import namedtuple

Contact = namedtuple("Contact", ["last_name", "first_name",
                                 "email", "phone"])
```

However, we still need to add a workaround to implement the validation of the fields. To address this common problem, we can use the `attrs` package available from the Python Package Index.

As usual, you can install it using the following command line with `pip`:

```
$ pip install attrs
```

Once installed, you can replace all the properties with the `attr.ib` descriptor. It also lets you specify a `validator` callback that takes the class instance, the attribute to be modified, and the value to be set.

With some minor modifications, we can rewrite our `Contact` class, reducing the number of lines of code by half:

```
import re
import attr
```

```
def required(message):
    def func(self, attr, val):
        if not val: raise ValueError(message)
    return func

def match(pattern, message):
    regex = re.compile(pattern)
    def func(self, attr, val):
        if val and not regex.match(val):
            raise ValueError(message)
    return func

@attr.s
class Contact(object):
    last_name = attr.ib(validator=required("Last name is required"))
    first_name = attr.ib(validator=required("First name is required"))
    email = attr.ib(validator=match(r"[^@]+@[^@]+\.[^@]+",
                                    "Invalid email format"))
    phone = attr.ib(validator=match(r"\([0-9]{3}\)\s[0-9]{7}",
                                    "Invalid phone format"))
```

When adding an external dependency in your projects, note not only the productivity benefits, but also other important aspects, such as documentation, support, and licensing.

You can find more information about the `attrs` package on its website at `http://www.attrs.org/en/stable/`.

Composing widgets to display information

It is difficult to build large applications if all the code is contained in a single class. By splitting the GUI code into specific classes, we can modularize the structure of our program and create widgets with well-defined purposes.

Getting ready

Apart from importing the Tkinter package, we will import the `Contact` class from the preceding recipe:

```
import tkinter as tk
import tkinter.messagebox as mb

from chapter5_01 import Contact
```

Verify that the `chapter5_01.py` file is in the same directory; otherwise, this `import-from` statement will raise `ImportError`.

How to do it...

We will create a scrollable list that will show all contacts. To represent each item in the list as a string, we will display the contact's last and first names:

```
class ContactList(tk.Frame):
    def __init__(self, master, **kwargs):
        super().__init__(master)
        self.lb = tk.Listbox(self, **kwargs)
        scroll = tk.Scrollbar(self, command=self.lb.yview)

        self.lb.config(yscrollcommand=scroll.set)
        scroll.pack(side=tk.RIGHT, fill=tk.Y)
        self.lb.pack(side=tk.LEFT, fill=tk.BOTH, expand=1)

    def insert(self, contact, index=tk.END):
        text = "{}, {}".format(contact.last_name, contact.first_name)
        self.lb.insert(index, text)

    def delete(self, index):
        self.lb.delete(index, index)

    def update(self, contact, index):
        self.delete(index)
        self.insert(contact, index)

    def bind_doble_click(self, callback):
        handler = lambda _: callback(self.lb.curselection()[0])
        self.lb.bind("<Double-Button-1>", handler)
```

To display and allow us to edit the details of a contact, we will also create a specific form. We will take the `LabelFrame` widget as a base class, with a `Label` and an `Entry` for each field:

```
class ContactForm(tk.LabelFrame):
    fields = ("Last name", "First name", "Email", "Phone")

    def __init__(self, master, **kwargs):
        super().__init__(master, text="Contact",
                         padx=10, pady=10, **kwargs)
        self.frame = tk.Frame(self)
        self.entries = list(map(self.create_field,
```

```
        enumerate(self.fields)))
    self.frame.pack()

def create_field(self, field):
    position, text = field
    label = tk.Label(self.frame, text=text)
    entry = tk.Entry(self.frame, width=25)
    label.grid(row=position, column=0, pady=5)
    entry.grid(row=position, column=1, pady=5)
    return entry

def load_details(self, contact):
    values = (contact.last_name, contact.first_name,
              contact.email, contact.phone)
    for entry, value in zip(self.entries, values):
        entry.delete(0, tk.END)
        entry.insert(0, value)

def get_details(self):
    values = [e.get() for e in self.entries]
    try:
        return Contact(*values)
    except ValueError as e:
        mb.showerror("Validation error", str(e), parent=self)

def clear(self):
    for entry in self.entries:
        entry.delete(0, tk.END)
```

How it works...

An important detail of the ContactList class is that it exposes the possibility to attach a callback to the double-click event. It also passes the clicked index as an argument to this function. We do this because we want to hide the implementation details of the underlying Listbox:

```
def bind_doble_click(self, callback):
    handler = lambda _: callback(self.lb.curselection()[0])
    self.lb.bind("<Double-Button-1>", handler)
```

ContactForm also offers an abstraction to instantiate a new contact from the values input in the entries:

```
def get_details(self):
    values = [e.get() for e in self.entries]
```

```
try:
    return Contact(*values)
except ValueError as e:
    mb.showerror("Validation error", str(e), parent=self)
```

Since we included field validations in our `Contact` class, instantiating a new contact might raise a `ValueError` if an entry contains an invalid value. To notify the user of this, we show an error dialog with the error message.

Reading records from a CSV file

As a first approach to loading read-only data into our application, we will use a **comma-separated values** (**CSV**) file. This format tabulates data in plain text files, where each file corresponds to the fields of a record, separated by commas, like so:

```
Gauford,Albertine,agauford0@acme.com, (614) 7171720
Greger,Bryce,bgreger1@acme.com, (616) 3543513
Wetherald,Rickey,rwetherald2@acme.com, (379) 3652495
```

This solution is easy to implement for simple scenarios, especially if the text fields do not contain line breaks. We will use the `csv` module from the standard library, and once the records are loaded into our application, we will populate the widgets developed in the previous recipes.

Getting ready

We will assemble the custom widgets we created in the previous recipe. Once the records are loaded from the CSV file, our application will look as shown in the following screenshot:

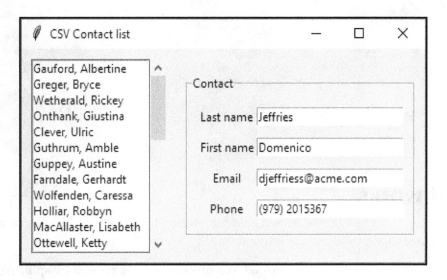

How to do it...

Apart from importing the Contact class, we will also import the ContactForm and ContactList widgets:

```python
import csv
import tkinter as tk

from chapter5_01 import Contact
from chapter5_02 import ContactForm, ContactList

class App(tk.Tk):
    def __init__(self):
        super().__init__()
        self.title("CSV Contact list")
        self.list = ContactList(self, height=12)
        self.form = ContactForm(self)
        self.contacts = self.load_contacts()

        for contact in self.contacts:
            self.list.insert(contact)
        self.list.pack(side=tk.LEFT, padx=10, pady=10)
        self.form.pack(side=tk.LEFT, padx=10, pady=10)
        self.list.bind_doble_click(self.show_contact)

    def load_contacts(self):
        with open("contacts.csv", encoding="utf-8", newline="") as f:
```

```
        return [Contact(*r) for r in csv.reader(f)]

    def show_contact(self, index):
        contact = self.contacts[index]
        self.form.load_details(contact)

if __name__ == "__main__":
    app = App()
    app.mainloop()
```

How it works...

The `load_contacts` function is responsible for reading the CSV file and transforming all the records into a list of `Contact` instances.

Each row read by `csv.reader` is returned as a tuple of strings, created by splitting the corresponding line using the comma delimiter. Since this tuple uses the same order as the parameters defined in the `__init__` method of the `Contact` class, we can simply unpack it with the `*` operator. This code can be summarized in a single line using a list comprehension, as follows:

```
def load_contacts(self):
    with open("contacts.csv", encoding="utf-8", newline="") as f:
        return [Contact(*r) for r in csv.reader(f)]
```

There is no problem in returning the list within the `with` block, since the context manager automatically closes the file when the method execution finishes.

Persisting data into a SQLite database

Since we want to be able to persist changes to the data through our application, we must implement a solution that serves both for reading and writing operations.

We could write all the records to the same plain text file we read them from after every modification, but this may be an ineffective solution when updating some records individually.

Since all the information is going to be stored locally, we can use a SQLite database to persist our application data. The `sqlite3` module is a part of the standard library, so you do not need any additional dependencies to start using it.

This recipe does not pretend to be a comprehensive guide to SQLite, but a practical introduction to integrate it into your Tkinter applications.

Getting ready

Before using the database in our application, we need to create and populate it with some initial data. All our contacts are stored in the CSV file, so we will use a migration script to read all the records and insert them into the database.

First, we create a connection to the `contacts.db` file, where our data will be stored. Then, we create the `contacts` table with the `last_name`, `first_name`, `email`, and `phone` text fields.

Since `csv.reader` returns an iterable of tuples whose fields follow the same order that we have defined in our `CREATE TABLE` statement, we can pass it directly to the `executemany` method. It will execute the `INSERT` statement for each tuple, replacing the question marks with the actual values of each record:

```python
import csv
import sqlite3

def main():
    with open("contacts.csv", encoding="utf-8", newline="") as f, \
            sqlite3.connect("contacts.db") as conn:
        conn.execute("""CREATE TABLE contacts (
                        last_name text,
                        first_name text,
                        email text,
                        phone text
                    )""")
        conn.executemany("INSERT INTO contacts VALUES (?,?,?,?)",
                        csv.reader(f))

if __name__ == "__main__":
    main()
```

The `with` statement automatically commits the transaction and closes both the file and the SQLite connection at the end of the execution.

How to do it...

To add new contacts to our database, we will define a `Toplevel` subclass that reuses `ContactForm` to instantiate a new contact:

```python
class NewContact(tk.Toplevel):
    def __init__(self, parent):
        super().__init__(parent)
        self.contact = None
        self.form = ContactForm(self)
        self.btn_add = tk.Button(self, text="Confirm",
                                    command=self.confirm)
        self.form.pack(padx=10, pady=10)
        self.btn_add.pack(pady=10)

    def confirm(self):
        self.contact = self.form.get_details()
        if self.contact:
            self.destroy()

    def show(self):
        self.grab_set()
        self.wait_window()
        return self.contact
```

The following top-level window will be displayed on top of the main window and returns the focus once the dialog is confirmed or closed:

We will also extend our `ContactForm` class with two additional buttons—one for updating the contact information, and another one for deleting the selected contact:

```python
class UpdateContactForm(ContactForm):
    def __init__(self, master, **kwargs):
        super().__init__(master, **kwargs)
        self.btn_save = tk.Button(self, text="Save")
        self.btn_delete = tk.Button(self, text="Delete")

        self.btn_save.pack(side=tk.RIGHT, ipadx=5, padx=5, pady=5)
        self.btn_delete.pack(side=tk.RIGHT, ipadx=5, padx=5, pady=5)

    def bind_save(self, callback):
        self.btn_save.config(command=callback)

    def bind_delete(self, callback):
        self.btn_delete.config(command=callback)
```

The `bind_save` and `bind_delete` methods allow us to attach a callback to the corresponding button's `command`.

To integrate all these changes, we will add the following code to our `App` class:

```python
class App(tk.Tk):
    def __init__(self, conn):
        super().__init__()
        self.title("SQLite Contacts list")
        self.conn = conn
        self.selection = None
        self.list = ContactList(self, height=15)
        self.form = UpdateContactForm(self)
        self.btn_new = tk.Button(self, text="Add new contact",
                                 command=self.add_contact)
        self.contacts = self.load_contacts()

        for contact in self.contacts:
            self.list.insert(contact)
        self.list.pack(side=tk.LEFT, padx=10, pady=10)
        self.form.pack(padx=10, pady=10)
        self.btn_new.pack(side=tk.BOTTOM, pady=5)

        self.list.bind_doble_click(self.show_contact)
        self.form.bind_save(self.update_contact)
        self.form.bind_delete(self.delete_contact)
```

We also need to modify the `load_contacts` method to create the contacts from a query result:

```python
def load_contacts(self):
    contacts = []
    sql = """SELECT rowid, last_name, first_name, email, phone
            FROM contacts"""
    for row in self.conn.execute(sql):
        contact = Contact(*row[1:])
        contact.rowid = row[0]
        contacts.append(contact)
    return contacts

def show_contact(self, index):
    self.selection = index
    contact = self.contacts[index]
    self.form.load_details(contact)
```

To add a contact to the list, we will instantiate a `NewContact` dialog and call its `show` method to get the details of the new contact. If these values are valid, we will store them in a tuple in the same order as they are specified in our `INSERT` statement:

```python
def to_values(self, c):
    return (c.last_name, c.first_name, c.email, c.phone)

def add_contact(self):
    new_contact = NewContact(self)
    contact = new_contact.show()
    if not contact:
        return
    values = self.to_values(contact)
    with self.conn:
        cursor = self.conn.cursor()
        cursor.execute("INSERT INTO contacts VALUES (?,?,?,?)",
        values)
        contact.rowid = cursor.lastrowid
    self.contacts.append(contact)
    self.list.insert(contact)
```

Once a contact is selected, we can update its details by retrieving the current form values. If they are valid, we execute an `UPDATE` statement to set the columns of the record with the specified `rowid`.

Since the fields of this statement are in the same order as the INSERT statement, we reuse the to_values method to create a tuple from the contact instance—the only difference is that we have to append the substitution parameter for rowid:

```python
def update_contact(self):
    if self.selection is None:
        return
    rowid = self.contacts[self.selection].rowid
    contact = self.form.get_details()
    if contact:
        values = self.to_values(contact)
        with self.conn:
            sql = """UPDATE contacts SET
                        last_name = ?,
                        first_name = ?,
                        email = ?,
                        phone = ?
                    WHERE rowid = ?"""
            self.conn.execute(sql, values + (rowid,))
        contact.rowid = rowid
        self.contacts[self.selection] = contact
        self.list.update(contact, self.selection)
```

To delete the selected contact, we get its rowid to replace it in our DELETE statement. Once the transaction is committed, the contact is removed from the GUI by clearing the form and deleting it from the list. The selection attribute is also set to None to avoid performing operations over an invalid selection:

```python
def delete_contact(self):
    if self.selection is None:
        return
    rowid = self.contacts[self.selection].rowid
    with self.conn:
        self.conn.execute("DELETE FROM contacts WHERE rowid = ?",
                          (rowid,))
    self.form.clear()
    self.list.delete(self.selection)
    self.selection = None
```

Finally, we will wrap the code to initialize our application in a main function:

```python
def main():
    with sqlite3.connect("contacts.db") as conn:
        app = App(conn)
        app.mainloop()

if __name__ == "__main__":
```

```
main()
```

With all these changes, our complete application will look as follows:

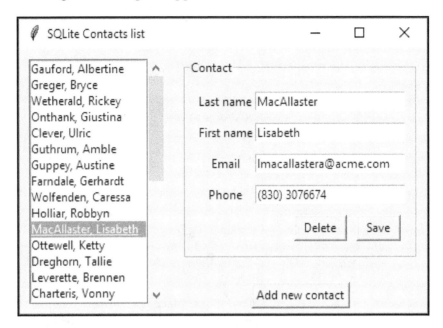

How it works...

This type of application is referred to using the **CRUD** acronym, which stands for **Create, Read, Update, and Delete**, and is easily mapped into the SQL statements INSERT, SELECT, UPDATE, and DELETE. We will now take a look at how to implement each operation using the sqlite3.Connection class.

INSERT statements add new records to a table, specifying the column names with the corresponding values. If you omit the column names, the column order will be used.

When you create a table in SQLite, it adds, by default, a column called rowid and automatically assigns a unique value to identify each row. Since we usually need it for subsequent operations, we retrieve it with the lastrowid attribute available in the Cursor class:

```
sql = "INSERT INTO my_table (col1, col2, col3) VALUES (?, ?, ?)"
with connection:
    cursor = connection.cursor()
```

```
    cursor.execute(sql, (value1, value2, value3))
    rowid = cursor.lastrowid
```

SELECT statements retrieve the values of one or more columns from the records of a table. Optionally, we can add a WHERE clause to filter the records to be retrieved. This is useful to efficiently implement searches and pagination, but we will omit this functionality in our sample application:

```
sql = "SELECT rowid, col1, col2, col3 FROM my_table"
for row in connection.execute(sql):
    # do something with row
```

UPDATE statements modify the value of one or more columns from the records in a table. Typically, we add a WHERE clause to update only the rows that match the given criteria—here, we could use rowid if we want to update a specific record:

```
sql = "UPDATE my_table SET col1 = ?, col2 = ?, col3 = ?
WHERE rowid = ?"
with connection:
    connection.execute(sql, (value1, value2, value3, rowid))
```

Finally, DELETE statements remove one or more records from a table. It is even more important to add the WHERE clause in these statements, because if we omit it, the statement will delete all the rows in the table:

```
sql = "DELETE FROM my_table WHERE rowid = ?"
with connection:
    connection.execute(sql, (rowid,))
```

See also

- The *Composing widgets to display information* recipe

Refactoring using the MVC pattern

Now that we have developed the complete functionality of our application, we can spot some problems in our current design. For instance, the App class has several responsibilities, from instantiating Tkinter widgets to executing SQL statements.

Although it seems easy and straightforward to write methods that perform an operation from end to end, this approach leads to code bases that are harder to maintain. We can detect this flaw by anticipating possible architectural changes, such as replacing our relational database with a REST backend accessed via HTTP.

Getting ready

Let's start by defining the MVC pattern and how it maps to the different parts of the application we built in our previous recipe.

This pattern divides our application into three components that encapsulate a single responsibility, forming the MVC triad:

- The **model** represents the domain data and contains the business rules to interact with it. In our example, it is the `Contact` class and the SQLite-specific code.
- The **view** is a graphical representation of the model data. In our case, it is made by the Tkinter widgets that compose the GUI.
- The **controller** connects the view and the model by receiving user input and updating the model data. This corresponds to our callbacks and event handlers and the attributes needed.

We will refactor our application to achieve this separation of concerns. You will note that the interactions between components require additional code, but they also help us to define their boundaries.

How to do it...

Firstly, we extract all the pieces of code that interact with the database into a separate class. This will allow us to hide the implementations details of our persistence layer, only exposing the four necessary methods, `get_contacts`, `add_contact`, `update_contact`, and `delete_contact`:

```
class ContactsRepository(object):
    def __init__(self, conn):
        self.conn = conn

    def to_values(self, c):
        return c.last_name, c.first_name, c.email, c.phone

    def get_contacts(self):
        sql = """SELECT rowid, last_name, first_name, email, phone
```

```
                    FROM contacts"""
         for row in self.conn.execute(sql):
             contact = Contact(*row[1:])
             contact.rowid = row[0]
             yield contact

     def add_contact(self, contact):
         sql = "INSERT INTO contacts VALUES (?, ?, ?, ?)"
         with self.conn:
             cursor = self.conn.cursor()
             cursor.execute(sql, self.to_values(contact))
             contact.rowid = cursor.lastrowid
         return contact

     def update_contact(self, contact):
         rowid = contact.rowid
         sql = """UPDATE contacts
                 SET last_name = ?, first_name = ?, email = ?,
                 phone = ?
                 WHERE rowid = ?"""
         with self.conn:
             self.conn.execute(sql, self.to_values(contact) + (rowid,))
         return contact

     def delete_contact(self, contact):
         sql = "DELETE FROM contacts WHERE rowid = ?"
         with self.conn:
             self.conn.execute(sql, (contact.rowid,))
```

This, alongside the `Contact` class, will compose our model.

Now, our view will simply contain the sufficient code to display the GUI and the methods to let the controller update it. We will also rename the class to `ContactsView` to better express its purpose:

```
class ContactsView(tk.Tk):
    def __init__(self):
        super().__init__()
        self.title("SQLite Contacts list")
        self.list = ContactList(self, height=15)
        self.form = UpdateContactForm(self)
        self.btn_new = tk.Button(self, text="Add new contact")

        self.list.pack(side=tk.LEFT, padx=10, pady=10)
        self.form.pack(padx=10, pady=10)
        self.btn_new.pack(side=tk.BOTTOM, pady=5)
```

```
    def set_ctrl(self, ctrl):
        self.btn_new.config(command=ctrl.create_contact)
        self.list.bind_doble_click(ctrl.select_contact)
        self.form.bind_save(ctrl.update_contact)
        self.form.bind_delete(ctrl.delete_contact)

    def add_contact(self, contact):
        self.list.insert(contact)

    def update_contact(self, contact, index):
        self.list.update(contact, index)

    def remove_contact(self, index):
        self.form.clear()
        self.list.delete(index)

    def get_details(self):
        return self.form.get_details()

    def load_details(self, contact):
        self.form.load_details(contact)
```

Note that user input is handled by the controller, so we added a `set_ctrl` method to connect it to the Tkinter callbacks.

Our `ContactsController` class will now contain all code missing from our initial `App` class, that is, the interactions between interface and persistence with the `selection` and `contacts` attributes:

```
class ContactsController(object):
    def __init__(self, repo, view):
        self.repo = repo
        self.view = view
        self.selection = None
        self.contacts = list(repo.get_contacts())

    def create_contact(self):
        new_contact = NewContact(self.view).show()
        if new_contact:
            contact = self.repo.add_contact(new_contact)
            self.contacts.append(contact)
            self.view.add_contact(contact)

    def select_contact(self, index):
        self.selection = index
        contact = self.contacts[index]
        self.view.load_details(contact)
```

```
def update_contact(self):
    if not self.selection:
        return
    rowid = self.contacts[self.selection].rowid
    update_contact = self.view.get_details()
    update_contact.rowid = rowid

    contact = self.repo.update_contact(update_contact)
    self.contacts[self.selection] = contact
    self.view.update_contact(contact, self.selection)

def delete_contact(self):
    if not self.selection:
        return
    contact = self.contacts[self.selection]
    self.repo.delete_contact(contact)
    self.view.remove_contact(self.selection)

def start(self):
    for c in self.contacts:
        self.view.add_contact(c)
    self.view.mainloop()
```

We will create a __main__.py script that will allow us not only to Bootstrap our application, but also to be able to launch it from a zipped file or with the name of the containing directory:

```
# Suppose that __main__.py is in the directory chapter5_05
$ python chapter5_05
# Or if we compress the directory contents
$ python chapter5_05.zip
```

How it works...

The original MVC implementation was introduced in the Smalltalk programming language, and it is represented by the following diagram:

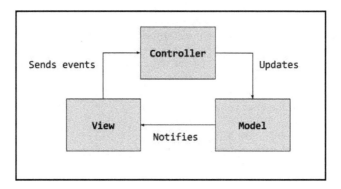

In the preceding diagram, we can see that the view passes user events to the controller, which in turn updates the model. To propagate these changes to the view, the model implements the **observer pattern**. This means that views subscribed to the model get notified when an update occurs, so they can query the model state and change the displayed data.

There is a variation of this design where there is no communication between the view and the model. Instead, changes to the view are made by the controller after it updates the model:

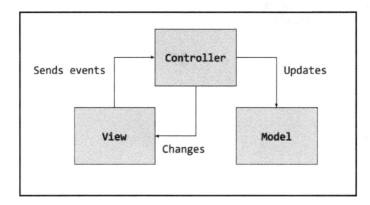

This approach is known as **passive model**, and it is the most common approach for modern MVC implementations—especially for web frameworks. We used this variation in our example because it simplifies our ContactsRepository and does not require major modifications to our ContactsController class.

There's more...

You might have noted that update and delete operations work thanks to the rowid field, for instance, in the update_contact method from the ContactsController class:

```
def update_contact(self):
    if not self.selection:
        return
    rowid = self.contacts[self.selection].rowid
    update_contact = self.view.get_details()
    update_contact.rowid = rowid
```

Since this is an implementation detail for our SQLite database, this should be hidden from the rest of our components.

A solution would be to add another field to the Contact class with a name such as id or contact_id—note that id is also a Python built-in function and some editors might incorrectly highlight it.

Then, we can assume this field is part of our domain data as a unique identifier and leave the implementation details of how it is generated to the model.

6
Asynchronous Programming

In this chapter, we will cover the following recipes:

- Scheduling actions
- Running methods on threads
- Performing HTTP requests
- Connecting threads with a progress bar
- Canceling scheduled actions
- Handling idle tasks
- Spawning separate processes

Introduction

Like any other programming language, Python lets you divide a process execution into multiple units that can be performed independently in time, called **threads**. When you launch a Python program, it starts its execution in the **main thread**.

Tkinter's main loop must start from the main thread, which is responsible for handling all the events and updates to the GUI. By default, our application code, such as callbacks and event handlers, will also be executed in this thread.

However, if we launch a long running action in this thread, the main thread execution will block until this operation is completed, and therefore the GUI will freeze and not respond to user events.

In this chapter, we will cover several recipes to achieve responsiveness in our applications while separate actions occur in the background, and also take a look at how to interact with them.

Scheduling actions

A basic technique to prevent blocking the main thread in Tkinter is scheduling an action that will be invoked after a timeout has elapsed.

In this recipe, we will take a look at how to implement this with Tkinter using the `after()` method, which can be called from all Tkinter widget classes.

Getting ready

The following code shows a straightforward example of how a callback can block the main loop.

This application consists of a single button that gets disabled when it is clicked, waits 5 seconds, and is enabled again. A trivial implementation would be the following one:

```python
import time
import tkinter as tk

class App(tk.Tk):
    def __init__(self):
        super().__init__()
        self.button = tk.Button(self, command=self.start_action,
                                text="Wait 5 seconds")
        self.button.pack(padx=20, pady=20)

    def start_action(self):
        self.button.config(state=tk.DISABLED)
        time.sleep(5)
        self.button.config(state=tk.NORMAL)

if __name__ == "__main__":
    app = App()
    app.mainloop()
```

If you run the preceding program, you will note that the **Wait 5 seconds** button is not disabled at all, but clicking on it freezes the GUI for 5 seconds. We can directly note that in the button styling, which looks active instead of disabled; also, the title bar will not respond to mouse clicks until the 5 seconds have elapsed:

If we had included additional widgets, such as entries and scroll bars, this would also have affected them.

We will now take a look at how to achieve the desired functionality by scheduling the action instead of suspending the thread execution.

How to do it...

The `after()` method allows you to register a callback that is invoked after a delay expressed in milliseconds within Tkinter's main loop. You can think of these registered alarms as events that should be handled as soon as the system is idle.

Therefore, we will replace the call to `time.sleep(5)` with `self.after(5000, callback)`. We use the `self` instance because the `after()` method is also available in the root `Tk` instance, and there will not be any difference in calling it from a child widget:

```python
import tkinter as tk

class App(tk.Tk):
    def __init__(self):
        super().__init__()
        self.button = tk.Button(self, command=self.start_action,
                                text="Wait 5 seconds")
        self.button.pack(padx=50, pady=20)

    def start_action(self):
        self.button.config(state=tk.DISABLED)
        self.after(5000, lambda: self.button.config(state=tk.NORMAL))

if __name__ == "__main__":
    app = App()
    app.mainloop()
```

With the preceding approach, the application is responsive before the scheduled action is called. The appearance of the button will change to disabled, and we could also interact with the title bar as usual:

How it works...

From the example mentioned in the preceding section, you might suppose the `after()` method executes the callback exactly after the given duration of milliseconds is passed as a delay.

However, what it does is request Tkinter to register an alarm that only guarantees that it will not be executed earlier than the specified time; so, if the main thread is busy, there is no upper limit to how long it will actually take.

We should also keep in mind that the method execution continues immediately after scheduling the action. The following example illustrates this behavior:

```
print("First")
self.after(1000, lambda: print("Third"))
print("Second")
```

The preceding snippet will print `"First"`, then `"Second"`, and finally `"Third"` after 1 second each. During this time, the main thread will keep the GUI responsive, and users can interact with the application as usual.

Usually, we would want to prevent the running of the same background action more than once, so it's a good idea to disable the widget that triggered the execution.

Do not forget that any scheduled function will be executed on the main thread, so just using `after()` is not enough to prevent freezing the GUI; it is also important to avoid executing long running methods as callbacks.

In the next recipe, we will take a look at how we can leverage the execution of these blocking actions in separate threads.

There's more...

The `after()` method returns an identifier of the scheduled alarm, which can be passed to the `after_cancel()` method to cancel the execution of the callback.

We will see in another recipe how to implement the functionality of stopping a scheduled callback using this method.

See also

- The *canceling scheduled actions* recipe

Running methods on threads

Since the main thread should be responsible only for updating the GUI and handling events, the rest of the background actions must be executed in separate threads.

Python's Standard Library includes the `threading` module to create and control multiple threads using a high-level interface that will allow us to work with simple classes and methods.

It is worth mentioning that CPython—the reference Python implementation—is inherently limited by the **GIL** (**Global Interpreter Lock**), a mechanism that prevents multiple threads from executing Python byte codes once and therefore, they cannot run in separate cores to take full advantage of multiprocessor systems. This should be kept in mind if trying to use the `threading` module to improve the performance of your application.

How to do it...

The following example combines the suspension of a thread with `time.sleep()` with an action scheduled via `after()`:

```
import time
import threading
import tkinter as tk

class App(tk.Tk):
    def __init__(self):
        super().__init__()
```

```
        self.button = tk.Button(self, command=self.start_action,
                                  text="Wait 5 seconds")
        self.button.pack(padx=50, pady=20)

    def start_action(self):
        self.button.config(state=tk.DISABLED)
        thread = threading.Thread(target=self.run_action)
        print(threading.main_thread().name)
        print(thread.name)
        thread.start()
        self.check_thread(thread)

    def check_thread(self, thread):
        if thread.is_alive():
            self.after(100, lambda: self.check_thread(thread))
        else:
            self.button.config(state=tk.NORMAL)

    def run_action(self):
        print("Starting long running action...")
        time.sleep(5)
        print("Long running action finished!")

if __name__ == "__main__":
    app = App()
    app.mainloop()
```

How it works...

To create a new `Thread` object, we can use the constructor with the `target` keyword argument, which will be invoked on a separate thread when we call its `start()` method.

In the preceding section, we used a reference to the `run_action` method on the current application instance:

```
thread = threading.Thread(target=self.run_action)
thread.start()
```

Then, we periodically polled the thread status using `after()`, which schedules the same method again until the thread is finished:

```
def check_thread(self, thread):
    if thread.is_alive():
        self.after(100, lambda: self.check_thread(thread))
    else:
```

```
self.button.config(state=tk.NORMAL)
```

In the preceding code snippet, we set a delay of `100` milliseconds, because there is no need to keep polling more frequently than that. Of course, this number may vary depending on the nature of the threaded action.

This timeline can be represented by the following sequence diagram:

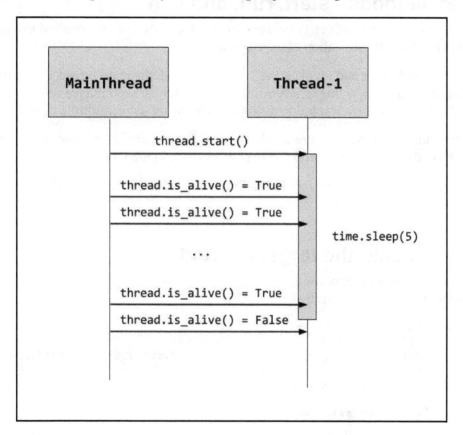

The rectangle on **Thread-1** represents the time it is busy executing **time.sleep(5)**. Meanwhile, **MainThread** only checks the status periodically, and there is no operation long enough to causes it to freeze the GUI.

There's more...

In this recipe, we had a brief introduction to the `Thread` class, but it is also important to point out some details about instantiating and using threads in your Python programs.

Thread methods - start, run, and join

In our example, we called `start()` because we wanted to execute the method in a separate thread and continue the execution of the current thread.

On the other hand, if we had invoked the `join()` method, the main thread would have been blocked until the new thread is terminated. Therefore, it would have caused the same "freezing" behavior that we wanted to avoid, even if we are using multiple threads.

Finally, the `run()` method is where the thread actually executes its callable target operation. We will override it when we extend the `Thread` class, as in the next recipe.

As a rule of thumb, always remember to call `start()` from the main thread to avoid blocking it.

Parameterizing the target method

When using the constructor of the `Thread` class, it's possible to specify the arguments of the target method via the `args` parameter:

```python
def start_action(self):
    self.button.config(state=tk.DISABLED)
    thread = threading.Thread(target=self.run_action, args=(5,))
    thread.start()
    self.check_thread(thread)

def run_action(self, timeout):
    # ...
```

Note that the `self` parameter is passed automatically since we are using the current instance to reference the target method. This might be handy in scenarios where the new thread needs to access information from the caller instance.

Performing HTTP requests

Communicating your application with a remote server via HTTP is a common use case of asynchronous programming. The client performs a request, which is transferred across the network using the TCP/IP protocol; then, the server processes the information and sends the response back to the client.

The time to perform this operation might vary from a few milliseconds to several seconds, but in most cases it is safe to assume that this latency may be noticed by your users.

Getting ready

There are plenty of third-party web services on the internet that can be freely accessed for prototyping purposes. However, we do not want to rely on an external service because its API may change or it might even go offline.

For this recipe, we will implement our custom HTTP server, which generates a random JSON response that will be printed on our separate GUI application:

```python
import time
import json
import random
from http.server import HTTPServer, BaseHTTPRequestHandler

class RandomRequestHandler(BaseHTTPRequestHandler):
    def do_GET(self):
        # Simulate latency
        time.sleep(3)

        # Write response headers
        self.send_response(200)
        self.send_header('Content-type', 'application/json')
        self.end_headers()

        # Write response body
        body = json.dumps({'random': random.random()})
        self.wfile.write(bytes(body, "utf8"))

def main():
    """Starts the HTTP server on port 8080"""
    server_address = ('', 8080)
    httpd = HTTPServer(server_address, RandomRequestHandler)
    httpd.serve_forever()
```

```
if __name__ == "__main__":
    main()
```

To start this server, run the `server.py` script and leave the process running to accept incoming HTTP requests on local port `8080`.

How to do it...

Our client application consists of a simple label to display information to users and a button to perform a new HTTP request to our local server:

```python
import json
import threading
import urllib.request
import tkinter as tk

class App(tk.Tk):
    def __init__(self):
        super().__init__()
        self.title("HTTP request example")
        self.label = tk.Label(self,
                              text="Click 'Start' to get a random
                              value")
        self.button = tk.Button(self, text="Start",
                                command=self.start_action)
        self.label.pack(padx=60, pady=10)
        self.button.pack(pady=10)

    def start_action(self):
        self.button.config(state=tk.DISABLED)
        thread = AsyncAction()
        thread.start()
        self.check_thread(thread)

    def check_thread(self, thread):
        if thread.is_alive():
            self.after(100, lambda: self.check_thread(thread))
        else:
            text = "Random value: {}".format(thread.result)
            self.label.config(text=text)
            self.button.config(state=tk.NORMAL)

class AsyncAction(threading.Thread):
    def run(self):
        self.result = None
        url = "http://localhost:8080"
```

```
        with urllib.request.urlopen(url) as f:
            obj = json.loads(f.read().decode("utf-8"))
            self.result = obj["random"]

if __name__ == "__main__":
    app = App()
    app.mainloop()
```

When the request is completed, the label shows the random value generated in the server, as follows:

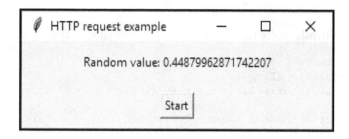

As usual, the button gets disabled while the asynchronous action is running to avoid performing a new request before the preceding one has been processed.

How it works...

In this recipe, we extended the `Thread` class to implement the logic that must run in a separate thread using a more object-oriented approach. This is done by overriding its `run()` method, which will be responsible for performing the HTTP request to the local server:

```
class AsyncAction(threading.Thread):
    def run(self):
        # ...
```

There are lots of HTTP client libraries, but here we will simply use the `urllib.request` module from the standard library. This module contains the `urlopen()` function, which can take a URL string and return an HTTP response that can work as a context manager—that is, it can be safely read and closed using the `with` statement.

The server returns a JSON document like the following one (you can check it by opening the `http://localhost:8080` URL in your browser):

```
{"random": 0.0915826359180778}
```

To decode the string to a object, we pass the response contents to the `loads()` function from the `json` module. Thanks to this, we can access the random value like using a dictionary, and store it in the `result` attribute, which is initialized to `None` to prevent the main thread from reading a field that is not set in case an error occurs:

```
def run(self):
    self.result = None
    url = "http://localhost:8080"
    with urllib.request.urlopen(url) as f:
        obj = json.loads(f.read().decode("utf-8"))
        self.result = obj["random"]
```

Then, the GUI periodically polls the thread status, as we saw in the preceding recipe:

```
def check_thread(self, thread):
    if thread.is_alive():
        self.after(100, lambda: self.check_thread(thread))
    else:
        text = "Random value: {}".format(thread.result)
        self.label.config(text=text)
        self.button.config(state=tk.NORMAL)
```

Here, the main difference is that once the thread is not alive, we can retrieve the value of the `result` attribute because it has been set before finishing its execution.

See also

- The *Running methods on threads* recipe

Connecting threads with a progress bar

Progress bars are useful indicators of the status of a background task, showing an incrementally filled portion of the bar relative to the progress. They are frequently used in long-running operations, so it is common to connect them with the threads that execute these tasks to provide visual feedback to end users.

Getting ready

Our sample application will consist of a horizontal progress bar that will increment a fixed amount of progress once the user clicks on the **Start** button:

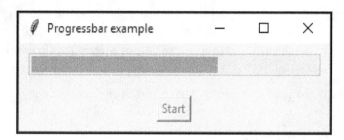

How to do it...

To simulate the execution of a background task, the increment of the progress bar will be generated from a different thread that will suspend its execution for 1 second between each step.

The communication will be made using a synchronized queue that allow us to exchange information in a thread-safe manner:

```python
import time
import queue
import threading
import tkinter as tk
import tkinter.ttk as ttk
import tkinter.messagebox as mb

class App(tk.Tk):
    def __init__(self):
        super().__init__()
        self.title("Progressbar example")
        self.queue = queue.Queue()
        self.progressbar = ttk.Progressbar(self, length=300,
                                            orient=tk.HORIZONTAL)
        self.button = tk.Button(self, text="Start",
                                command=self.start_action)

        self.progressbar.pack(padx=10, pady=10)
        self.button.pack(padx=10, pady=10)

    def start_action(self):
```

```
            self.button.config(state=tk.DISABLED)
            thread = AsyncAction(self.queue, 20)
            thread.start()
            self.poll_thread(thread)

        def poll_thread(self, thread):
            self.check_queue()
            if thread.is_alive():
                self.after(100, lambda: self.poll_thread(thread))
            else:
                self.button.config(state=tk.NORMAL)
                mb.showinfo("Done!", "Async action completed")

        def check_queue(self):
            while self.queue.qsize():
                try:
                    step = self.queue.get(0)
                    self.progressbar.step(step * 100)
                except queue.Empty:
                    pass

class AsyncAction(threading.Thread):
    def __init__(self, queue, steps):
        super().__init__()
        self.queue = queue
        self.steps = steps

    def run(self):
        for _ in range(self.steps):
            time.sleep(1)
            self.queue.put(1 / self.steps)

if __name__ == "__main__":
    app = App()
    app.mainloop()
```

How it works...

Progressbar is a themed widget included in the tkinter.ttk module. We will dive into this module in Chapter 8, *Themed Widgets*, to explore the new widgets that it defines, but so far we only need to use Progressbar as a regular widget.

We also need to import the `queue` module, which defines synchronized collections such as `Queue`. Synchronicity is an important topic in multithreaded environments, because an unexpected result might occur if shared resources are accessed at exactly the same time—we define this unlikely but possible scenarios as a **race condition**.

With these additions, our `App` class contains these new statements:

```
# ...
import queue
import tkinter.ttk as ttk

class App(tk.Tk):
    def __init__(self):
        # ...
        self.queue = queue.Queue()
        self.progressbar = ttk.Progressbar(self, length=300,
                                            orient=tk.HORIZONTAL)
```

Like previous examples, the `start_action()` method starts a thread, passing the queue and the number of steps that will simulate the long running task:

```
def start_action(self):
    self.button.config(state=tk.DISABLED)
    thread = AsyncAction(self.queue, 20)
    thread.start()
    self.poll_thread(thread)
```

Our `AsyncAction` subclass defines a custom constructor to receive these parameters, which will later be used in the `run()` method:

```
class AsyncAction(threading.Thread):
    def __init__(self, queue, steps):
        super().__init__()
        self.queue = queue
        self.steps = steps

    def run(self):
        for _ in range(self.steps):
            time.sleep(1)
            self.queue.put(1 / self.steps)
```

The loop suspends the execution of the thread for 1 second and adds the increment to the queue as many times as indicated in the `steps` attribute.

The item added to the queue is retrieved from the application instance by reading the queue from `check_queue()`:

```
def check_queue(self):
    while self.queue.qsize():
        try:
            step = self.queue.get(0)
            self.progressbar.step(step * 100)
        except queue.Empty:
            pass
```

The following method is periodically called from `poll_thread()`, which polls the thread status and schedules itself again with `after()` until the thread completes its execution:

```
def poll_thread(self, thread):
    self.check_queue()
    if thread.is_alive():
        self.after(100, lambda: self.poll_thread(thread))
    else:
        self.button.config(state=tk.NORMAL)
        mb.showinfo("Done!", "Async action completed")
```

See also

- The *Running methods on threads* recipe

Canceling scheduled actions

Tkinter's scheduling mechanism not only provides methods to delay callback executions, but also to cancel them if they have not been executed yet. Consider an operation that may take too much time to complete, so we want to let users to stop it by pressing a button or closing the application.

Getting ready

We will take the example from the first recipe and add a **Stop** button to allow us to cancel the scheduled action.

This button will be enabled only while the action is scheduled, which means that once you click on the left button, the user can wait for 5 seconds, or click on the **Stop** button to immediately enable it again:

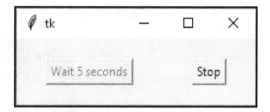

How to do it...

The `after_cancel()` method cancels the execution of a scheduled action by taking the identifier previously returned by calling `after()`. In this example, this value is stored in the `scheduled_id` attribute:

```python
import time
import tkinter as tk

class App(tk.Tk):
    def __init__(self):
        super().__init__()
        self.button = tk.Button(self, command=self.start_action,
                                 text="Wait 5 seconds")
        self.cancel = tk.Button(self, command=self.cancel_action,
                                 text="Stop", state=tk.DISABLED)
        self.button.pack(padx=30, pady=20, side=tk.LEFT)
        self.cancel.pack(padx=30, pady=20, side=tk.LEFT)

    def start_action(self):
        self.button.config(state=tk.DISABLED)
        self.cancel.config(state=tk.NORMAL)
        self.scheduled_id = self.after(5000, self.init_buttons)

    def init_buttons(self):
        self.button.config(state=tk.NORMAL)
        self.cancel.config(state=tk.DISABLED)

    def cancel_action(self):
        print("Canceling scheduled", self.scheduled_id)
        self.after_cancel(self.scheduled_id)
        self.init_buttons()
```

```
if __name__ == "__main__":
    app = App()
    app.mainloop()
```

How it works...

To unschedule a callback, we will first need the alarm identifier returned by `after()`. We will store this identifier in the `scheduled_id` attribute, since we will need it in a separate method:

```
def start_action(self):
    self.button.config(state=tk.DISABLED)
    self.cancel.config(state=tk.NORMAL)
    self.scheduled_id = self.after(5000, self.init_buttons)
```

Then, this field is passed to `after_cancel()` in the callback of the `Stop` button:

```
def cancel_action(self):
    print("Canceling scheduled", self.scheduled_id)
    self.after_cancel(self.scheduled_id)
    self.init_buttons()
```

In our case, it is important to disable the `Start` button once it is clicked, because if `start_action()` is called twice, `scheduled_id` would be overridden, and the `Stop` button could only cancel the last scheduled action.

As a side note, `after_cancel()` has no effect if we call it with an alarm identifier that has already been executed.

There's more...

In this section, we covered how to cancel a scheduled alarm, but if this callback was polling the status of a background thread, you might wonder how to stop the thread as well.

Unfortunately, there is no official API to gracefully stop a `Thread` instance. If you have defined a custom subclass, you might need to include a flag that is periodically checked inside its `run()` method:

```
class MyAsyncAction(threading.Thread):
    def __init__(self):
        super().__init__()
        self.do_stop = False
```

```
def run(self):
    # Start execution...
    if not self.do_stop:
        # Continue execution...
```

Then, this flag can be externally modified by setting `thread.do_stop = True` when invoking `after_cancel()` also to stop the thread.

Obviously, this approach will heavily depend on the operations performed inside the `run()` method—for instance, this mechanism is easier to implement if it consists of a loop, because you can perform this check between each iteration.

Starting from Python 3.4, you can use the `asyncio` module, which includes classes and functions to manage asynchronous operations, including cancellations. Even though this module is outside the scope of this book, we recommend you explore it if you face more complex scenarios.

Handling idle tasks

There are certain situations where an operation causes a small pause in the execution of the program. It might not even take a second to complete, but it is still noticeable to your users because it introduces a momentary pause in the GUI.

In this recipe, we will discuss how to deal with these scenarios without needing to process the whole task in a separate thread.

Getting ready

We will take the example from the *Scheduling actions* recipe, but with a timeout of 1 second instead of 5.

How to do it...

When we change the state of the button to `DISABLED`, the callback continues its execution, so the state of the button is not actually changed until the system is idle, which means it has to wait for `time.sleep()` to complete.

However, we can force Tkinter to update all the pending GUI updates to execute at a specific moment, as shown in the following script:

```python
import time
import tkinter as tk

class App(tk.Tk):
    def __init__(self):
        super().__init__()
        self.button = tk.Button(self, command=self.start_action,
                                text="Wait 1 second")
        self.button.pack(padx=30, pady=20)

    def start_action(self):
        self.button.config(state=tk.DISABLED)
        self.update_idletasks()
        time.sleep(1)
        self.button.config(state=tk.NORMAL)

if __name__ == "__main__":
    app = App()
    app.mainloop()
```

How it works...

The key to the snippet mentioned in the preceding section is the call to `self.update_idletasks()`. Thanks to this, the change to the button state is processed by Tkinter before calling `time.sleep()`. So, during the second that the callback is suspended, the button has the desired appearance, instead of `ACTIVE`, which is the state that Tkinter sets for the button before invoking the callback.

We used `time.sleep()` to illustrate a situation where a statement takes long enough to execute but is short enough to consider moving it to a new thread—in real-world scenarios, it would be a more complex computing operation.

Spawning separate processes

Under some circumstances, it is not possible to implement the desired functionality for your application just by using threads. For instance, you might want to call a separate program that could be written in a different language.

In this case, we also need to use the `subprocess` module to invoke the target program from our Python process.

Getting ready

The following example performs a ping to an indicated DNS or IP address:

How to do it...

As usual, we define a custom `AsyncAction` method, but, in this case, we call `subprocess.run()` with the value set in the Entry widget.

This function starts a separate subprocess that, unlike threads, uses a separate memory space. This means that in order to get the result of the `ping` command, we must pipe the result printed to the standard output and read it in our Python program:

```
import threading
import subprocess
import tkinter as tk

class App(tk.Tk):
    def __init__(self):
```

```
            super().__init__()
            self.entry = tk.Entry(self)
            self.button = tk.Button(self, text="Ping!",
                                    command=self.do_ping)
            self.output = tk.Text(self, width=80, height=15)
            self.entry.grid(row=0, column=0, padx=5, pady=5)
            self.button.grid(row=0, column=1, padx=5, pady=5)
            self.output.grid(row=1, column=0, columnspan=2,
                             padx=5, pady=5)

        def do_ping(self):
            self.button.config(state=tk.DISABLED)
            thread = AsyncAction(self.entry.get())
            thread.start()
            self.poll_thread(thread)

        def poll_thread(self, thread):
            if thread.is_alive():
                self.after(100, lambda: self.poll_thread(thread))
            else:
                self.button.config(state=tk.NORMAL)
                self.output.delete(1.0, tk.END)
                self.output.insert(tk.END, thread.result)

    class AsyncAction(threading.Thread):
        def __init__(self, ip):
            super().__init__()
            self.ip = ip

        def run(self):
            self.result = subprocess.run(["ping", self.ip], shell=True,
                                         stdout=subprocess.PIPE).stdout

    if __name__ == "__main__":
        app = App()
        app.mainloop()
```

How it works...

The run() function executes the subprocess specified in the array of arguments. By default, the result contains only the return code of the process, so we also pass the stdout option with the PIPE constant to indicate that the standard output stream should be piped.

We call this function with the keyword argument—shell—set to True to avoid opening a new console for the ping subprocess:

```
def run(self):
    self.result = subprocess.run(["ping", self.ip], shell=True,
                             stdout=subprocess.PIPE).stdout
```

Finally, when the main thread verifies that this operation has finished, it prints the output to the Text widget:

```
def poll_thread(self, thread):
    if thread.is_alive():
        self.after(100, lambda: self.poll_thread(thread))
    else:
        self.button.config(state=tk.NORMAL)
        self.output.delete(1.0, tk.END)
        self.output.insert(tk.END, thread.result)
```

Canvas and Graphics 7

In this chapter, we will cover the following recipes:

- Understanding the coordinate system
- Drawing lines and arrows
- Writing text on a canvas
- Adding shapes to the canvas
- Finding items by their position
- Moving canvas items
- Detecting collisions between items
- Deleting items from a canvas
- Binding events to canvas items
- Rendering a canvas into a PostScript file

Introduction

In the first chapter, we covered several recipes for the standard Tkinter widget. However, we skipped the **Canvas** widget because it offers plenty of graphical capabilities, and it deserves a dedicated chapter by itself to dive into its common use cases.

A canvas is a rectangular area where you can not only display text and geometric shapes, such as lines, rectangles, or ovals, but also nest other Tkinter widgets. These objects are called **canvas items**, and each one has a unique identifier that allows us to manipulate them before they are initially displayed on the canvas.

We will cover the methods of the `Canvas` class with interactive samples, which will help us to identify frequent patterns that could be translated to the applications we want to build.

Understanding the coordinate system

To draw graphic items on a canvas, we will need to specify their position using a **coordinate system**. Since a canvas is a two-dimensional space, points will be notated by their coordinates on the horizontal and vertical axes—commonly labeled x and y respectively.

With a simple application, we can easily illustrate how to locate these points in relation to the origin of the coordinate system, placed in the upper-left corner of the canvas area.

How to do it...

The following program contains an empty canvas and a label that shows the location of the cursor on the canvas; you can move the cursor to see what position it is placed in, giving clear feedback on how the x and y coordinates increment or decrement, depending on the direction you move the mouse pointer:

```python
import tkinter as tk

class App(tk.Tk):
    def __init__(self):
        super().__init__()
        self.title("Basic canvas")

        self.canvas = tk.Canvas(self, bg="white")
        self.label = tk.Label(self)
        self.canvas.bind("<Motion>", self.mouse_motion)

        self.canvas.pack()
        self.label.pack()

    def mouse_motion(self, event):
        x, y = event.x, event.y
        text = "Mouse position: ({}, {})".format(x, y)
        self.label.config(text=text)

if __name__ == "__main__":
    app = App()
    app.mainloop()
```

How it works...

The `Canvas` instance is created like any other Tkinter widget, that is, by first passing the parent container and the additional configuration options as keyword arguments:

```
def __init__(self):
    # ...
    self.canvas = tk.Canvas(self, bg="white")
    self.label = tk.Label(self)
    self.canvas.bind("<Motion>", self.mouse_motion)
```

The next screenshot shows a point composed of the perpendicular projections of each axis:

- The x coordinate corresponds to the distance on the horizontal axis and increments its value when you move the cursor from left to right
- The y coordinate is the distance on the vertical axis and increments its value when you move the cursor from up to down

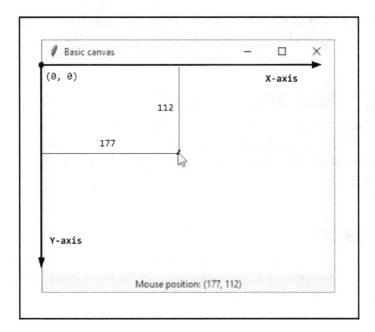

As you might have noticed in the preceding screenshot, these coordinates directly map to the x and y attributes of the event instance passed to the handler:

```
def mouse_motion(self, event):
    x, y = event.x, event.y
    text = "Mouse position: ({}, {})".format(x, y)
    self.label.config(text=text)
```

This happens because these attributes are calculated in respect to the widget that the event is bound to, in this case, the <Motion> sequence.

There's more...

The canvas surface can also display items with negative values in their coordinates. Depending on the item size, they can be partially shown on the top or left borders of the canvas.

In a similar way, if an item is placed at a point where any of its coordinates is greater than the canvas size, it may partially fall outside the bottom or right borders.

Drawing lines and arrows

One of the most basic actions you can perform with a canvas is drawing segments from one point to another. Although it is possible to directly draw polygons using other methods, the create_line method of the Canvas class has enough options to understand the basics of displaying items.

Getting ready

In this recipe, we will build an application that allows us to draw lines by clicking on the canvas. Each line will be displayed by clicking first on the point that will determine the line start, and a second time to set the line end.

We will be also able to specify some appearance options, such as color and width:

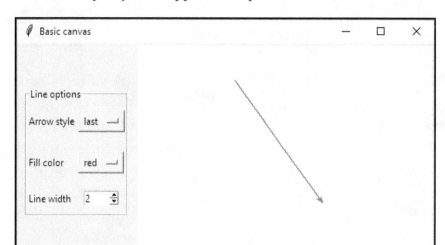

How to do it...

Our `App` class will be responsible for creating an empty canvas and handling mouse click events.

The information on the line options will be retrieved from the `LineForm` class. The approach of separating this component into a different class helps us to abstract its implementation details and focus on how to work with the `Canvas` widget.

For the sake of brevity, we omit the implementation of the `LineForm` class in the following snippet:

```python
import tkinter as tk

class LineForm(tk.LabelFrame):
    # ...

class App(tk.Tk):
    def __init__(self):
        super().__init__()
        self.title("Basic canvas")

        self.line_start = None
        self.form = LineForm(self)
```

```
        self.canvas = tk.Canvas(self, bg="white")
        self.canvas.bind("<Button-1>", self.draw)

        self.form.pack(side=tk.LEFT, padx=10, pady=10)
        self.canvas.pack(side=tk.LEFT)

    def draw(self, event):
        x, y = event.x, event.y
        if not self.line_start:
            self.line_start = (x, y)
        else:
            x_origin, y_origin = self.line_start
            self.line_start = None
            line = (x_origin, y_origin, x, y)
            arrow = self.form.get_arrow()
            color = self.form.get_color()
            width = self.form.get_width()
            self.canvas.create_line(*line, arrow=arrow,
                                    fill=color, width=width)

if __name__ == "__main__":
    app = App()
    app.mainloop()
```

You can find the complete code sample in the `chapter7_02.py` file.

How it works...

Since we want to handle the mouse clicks on the canvas, we will bind the `draw()` method to this type of event. We will also define the `line_start` field

to keep track of the start point of each new line:

```
    def __init__(self):
        # ...

        self.line_start = None
        self.form = LineForm(self)
        self.canvas = tk.Canvas(self, bg="white")
        self.canvas.bind("<Button-1>", self.draw)
```

The `draw()` method contains the main logic of our application. The first click on each new line serves to determine the origin and does not perform any drawing operation. These coordinates are retrieved from the `event` object passed to the handler:

```
def draw(self, event):
    x, y = event.x, event.y
    if not self.line_start:
        self.line_start = (x, y)
    else:
        # ...
```

If `line_start` already has a value, we retrieve the origin point and pass it with the coordinates of the current event to draw the line:

```
def draw(self, event):
    x, y = event.x, event.y
    if not self.line_start:
        # ...
    else:
        x_origin, y_origin = self.line_start
        self.line_start = None
        line = (x_origin, y_origin, x, y)
        self.canvas.create_line(*line)
        text = "Line drawn from ({}, {}) to ({}, {})".format(*line)
```

The `canvas.create_line()` method takes four arguments, where the first two are the horizontal and vertical coordinates of the line start and the last two are the coordinates corresponding to the line end.

Writing text on a canvas

In case we want to write some text on a canvas, we do not need to use an additional widget, such as a Label. The `Canvas` class includes the `create_text` method to display a string that can be manipulated the same as any other type of canvas item.

It is also possible to use the same formatting options that we can specify to add style to the text of regular Tkinter widgets, such as color, font family, and size.

Getting ready

In this example, we will connect an Entry widget with the contents of a text canvas item. While the input will have the standard appearance, the text on the canvas will have a customized style:

How to do it...

The text item will be initially displayed using the `canvas.create_text()` method, with some additional options to use a Consolas font and a blue color.

The dynamic behavior of the text item will be implemented using `StringVar`. By tracing this Tkinter variable, we can modify the contents of the item:

```python
import tkinter as tk

class App(tk.Tk):
    def __init__(self):
        super().__init__()
        self.title("Canvas text items")
        self.geometry("300x100")

        self.var = tk.StringVar()
        self.entry = tk.Entry(self, textvariable=self.var)
        self.canvas = tk.Canvas(self, bg="white")

        self.entry.pack(pady=5)
        self.canvas.pack()
        self.update()

        w, h = self.canvas.winfo_width(), self.canvas.winfo_height()
        options = { "font": "courier", "fill": "blue",
                    "activefill": "red" }
        self.text_id = self.canvas.create_text((w/2, h/2), **options)
```

```
        self.var.trace("w", self.write_text)

    def write_text(self, *args):
        self.canvas.itemconfig(self.text_id, text=self.var.get())

if __name__ == "__main__":
    app = App()
    app.mainloop()
```

You can try out this program by typing some arbitrary text on the entry input and noticing how it automatically updates the text on the canvas.

How it works...

First, we initialize the `Entry` instance with its `StringVar` variable and the Canvas widget:

```
self.var = tk.StringVar()
self.entry = tk.Entry(self, textvariable=self.var)
self.canvas = tk.Canvas(self, bg="white")
```

Then, we place the widgets by calling the methods for the Pack geometry manager. Note the importance of calling `update()` on the root window, because we want to force Tkinter to process all the pending changes, in this case rendering the widgets before the __init__ method continues its execution:

```
self.entry.pack(pady=5)
self.canvas.pack()
self.update()
```

We did this because the next step will be to calculate the canvas dimensions, and until the geometry manager has displayed the widget, it will not have the real values of its width and height.

After this, we can safely retrieve the canvas dimensions. Since we want to align the text item with the center of the canvas, we divide the values of width and height by half.

These coordinates determine the position of the item, and together with the styling options, are passed to the `create_text()` method. The `text` keyword argument is a common option used here, but we will omit it because it will be dynamically set when `StringVar` changes its value:

```
w, h = self.canvas.winfo_width(), self.canvas.winfo_height()
options = { "font": "courier", "fill": "blue",
            "activefill": "red" }
```

```
self.text_id = self.canvas.create_text((w/2, h/2), **options)
self.var.trace("w", self.write_text)
```

The identifier returned by `create_text()` is stored in the `text_id` field. It will be used on the `write_text()` method to reference the item, which is invoked by the tracing mechanism on write operations of the `var` instance.

To update the `text` option inside the `write_text()` handler, we call the `canvas.itemconfig()` method with the item identifier as the first argument, and then the configuration options.

In our case, we use the `text_id` field that we stored while initializing our `App` instance and the contents of `StringVar` via its `get()` method:

```
def write_text(self, *args):
    self.canvas.itemconfig(self.text_id, text=self.var.get())
```

We defined our `write_text()` method so that it can receive a variable number of arguments even though we do not need them, because the `trace()` method of Tkinter variables passes them to the callback functions.

There's more...

The `canvas.create_text()` method has many other options to customize the created canvas items.

Placing the text by its upper-left corner

The `anchor` option allow us to control where to place the item relative to the position passed as its first argument to `canvas.create_text()`. By default, this option value is `tk.CENTER`, which means that the text widget is centered on these coordinates.

If you want to place the text on the upper-left corner of the canvas, you can do so by passing the `(0, 0)` position and setting the `anchor` option to `tk.NW`, aligning the origin to the north-west of the rectangular area the text is placed within:

```
# ...
options = { "font": "courier", "fill": "blue",
            "activefill": "red", "anchor": tk.NW }
self.text_id = self.canvas.create_text((0, 0), **options)
```

The preceding code snippet will give us the following result:

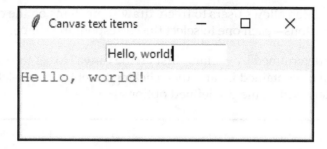

Setting line wrapping

By default, the contents of a text item will be displayed in a single line. The `width` option allows us to define a maximum line width, which wraps lines longer than that:

```
# ...
options = { "font": "courier", "fill": "blue",
            "activefill": "red", "width": 70 }
self.text_id = self.canvas.create_text((w/2, h/2), **options)
```

Now, when we write `Hello, world!` on the entry, the part of the text that exceeds the line width will be displayed in a new line:

Adding shapes to the canvas

In this recipe, we will cover three of the standard canvas items: rectangles, ovals, and arcs. All of them are displayed within a bounding box, so the use of only two points is necessary to set their position: the upper-left corner of the box and the lower-right corner.

Getting ready

The following application allows users to freely draw some items on the canvas by selecting its type with three buttons—each one to select the corresponding shape.

Item's positions are determined by clicking first on the canvas to set the upper-left corner of the box the item will be contained in, and then clicking to set the lower-left corner of this box and draw the item with some predefined options:

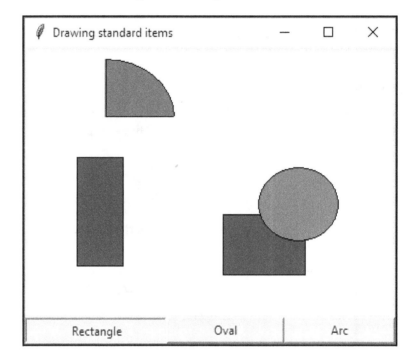

How to do it...

Our application stores the currently chosen type of item, which is selected with one of the three buttons placed on a frame below the canvas.

Clicking with the primary mouse button on the canvas triggers the handler that stores the position of the first corner of the new item, and once it is clicked again, it reads the value of the selected shape to conditionally draw the corresponding item:

```
import tkinter as tk
from functools import partial
```

```
class App(tk.Tk):
    shapes = ("rectangle", "oval", "arc")
    def __init__(self):
        super().__init__()
        self.title("Drawing standard items")

        self.start = None
        self.shape = None
        self.canvas = tk.Canvas(self, bg="white")
        frame = tk.Frame(self)
        for shape in self.shapes:
            btn = tk.Button(frame, text=shape.capitalize())
            btn.config(command=partial(self.set_selection, btn, shape))
            btn.pack(side=tk.LEFT, expand=True, fill=tk.BOTH)

        self.canvas.bind("<Button-1>", self.draw_item)
        self.canvas.pack()
        frame.pack(fill=tk.BOTH)

    def set_selection(self, widget, shape):
        for w in widget.master.winfo_children():
            w.config(relief=tk.RAISED)
        widget.config(relief=tk.SUNKEN)
        self.shape = shape

    def draw_item(self, event):
        x, y = event.x, event.y
        if not self.start:
            self.start = (x, y)
        else:
            x_origin, y_origin = self.start
            self.start = None
            bbox = (x_origin, y_origin, x, y)
            if self.shape == "rectangle":
                self.canvas.create_rectangle(*bbox, fill="blue",
                                             activefill="yellow")
            elif self.shape == "oval":
                self.canvas.create_oval(*bbox, fill="red",
                                        activefill="yellow")
            elif self.shape == "arc":
                self.canvas.create_arc(*bbox, fill="green",
                                       activefill="yellow")

if __name__ == "__main__":
    app = App()
    app.mainloop()
```

How it works...

To dynamically select the type of item drawn by clicking on the canvas, we will create a button for each one of the shapes by iterating over the `shapes` tuple.

We define each callback command using the `partial` function from the `functools` module. Thanks to this, we can freeze the `Button` instance and the current shape of the loop as arguments to the callback of each button:

```
for shape in self.shapes:
    btn = tk.Button(frame, text=shape.capitalize())
    btn.config(command=partial(self.set_selection, btn, shape))
    btn.pack(side=tk.LEFT, expand=True, fill=tk.BOTH)
```

The `set_selection()` callback marks the clicked button with the SUNKEN relief and stores the selection in the `shape` field.

The other widget siblings are configured with the standard relief (RAISED) by navigating to the parent, available in the `master` field of the current widget, and then retrieving all the children widgets with the `winfo_children()` method:

```
def set_selection(self, widget, shape):
    for w in widget.master.winfo_children():
        w.config(relief=tk.RAISED)
    widget.config(relief=tk.SUNKEN)
    self.shape = shape
```

The `draw_item()` handler stores the coordinates of the first click of each pair of events to draw the item when the canvas is clicked again—exactly like we previously did in the *Drawing lines and arrows* recipe.

Depending on the value of the `shape` field, one of the following methods is invoked to display the corresponding item type:

- `canvas.create_rectangle(x0, y0, x1, y1, **options)`: Draws a rectangle whose upper-left corner is placed at **(x0, y0)** and lower-right corner at **(x1, y1)**:

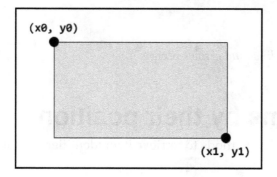

- `canvas.create_oval(x0, y0, x1, y1, **options)`: Draws an ellipse that fits into the rectangle from **(x0, y0)** to **(x1, y1)**:

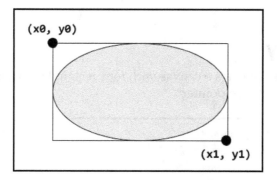

- `canvas.create_arc(x0, y0, x1, y1, **options)`: Draws a quarter of the ellipse that would fit into the rectangle from **(x0, y0)** to **(x1, y1)**:

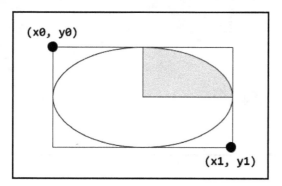

See also

- The *Drawing lines and arrows* recipe

Finding items by their position

The `Canvas` class includes methods to retrieve item identifiers that are close to a canvas coordinate.

This is very useful because it saves us from storing each reference to a canvas item and then calculating their current position to detect which ones are within a specific area or closest to a certain point.

Getting ready

The following application creates a canvas with four rectangles, and changes the color of the one that is closest to the mouse pointer:

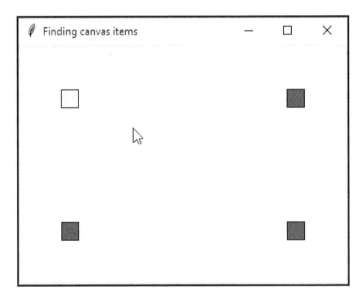

How to do it...

To find the closest item to the pointer, we pass the mouse event coordinates to the `canvas.find_closest()` method, which retrieves the identifier of the item that is closest to the given position.

Once there is at least one item in the canvas, we can safely assume that this method will always return a valid item identifier:

```python
import tkinter as tk

class App(tk.Tk):
    def __init__(self):
        super().__init__()
        self.title("Finding canvas items")

        self.current = None
        self.canvas = tk.Canvas(self, bg="white")
        self.canvas.bind("<Motion>", self.mouse_motion)
        self.canvas.pack()

        self.update()
        w = self.canvas.winfo_width()
        h = self.canvas.winfo_height()
        positions = [(60, 60), (w-60, 60), (60, h-60), (w-60, h-60)]
        for x, y in positions:
            self.canvas.create_rectangle(x-10, y-10, x+10, y+10,
                                         fill="blue")

    def mouse_motion(self, event):
        self.canvas.itemconfig(self.current, fill="blue")
        self.current = self.canvas.find_closest(event.x, event.y)
        self.canvas.itemconfig(self.current, fill="yellow")

if __name__ == "__main__":
    app = App()
    app.mainloop()
```

How it works...

During application initialization, we create the canvas and define the `current` field to store a reference to the current highlighted item. We also handle the "`<Motion>`" events on the canvas with the `mouse_motion()` method:

```
self.current = None
self.canvas = tk.Canvas(self, bg="white")
self.canvas.bind("<Motion>", self.mouse_motion)
self.canvas.pack()
```

Then, we create four items with a specific arrangement so that we can easily visualize the item that is closest to the mouse pointer:

```
self.update()
w = self.canvas.winfo_width()
h = self.canvas.winfo_height()
positions = [(60, 60), (w-60, 60), (60, h-60), (w-60, h-60)]
for x, y in positions:
    self.canvas.create_rectangle(x-10, y-10, x+10, y+10,
                                 fill="blue")
```

The `mouse_motion()` handler sets the color of the current item back to `blue` and saves the item identifier of the new one, which is closer to the event coordinates. Finally, the `fill` color of this item is set to `yellow`:

```
def mouse_motion(self, event):
    self.canvas.itemconfig(self.current, fill="blue")
    self.current = self.canvas.find_closest(event.x, event.y)
    self.canvas.itemconfig(self.current, fill="yellow")
```

Initially, there are no errors when `mouse_motion()` is called for the first time and the `current` field is still `None`, since it is also a valid input parameter to `itemconfig()`; it just does not perform any action on the canvas.

Moving canvas items

Once placed, canvas items can be moved to a certain offset, without having to specify the absolute coordinates.

When moving canvas items, it is usually relevant to calculate its current position, for instance, to determine whether they are placed inside a concrete canvas area, and restrict their movements so that they always stay within that area.

How to do it...

Our example will consist of a simple canvas with a rectangle item, which can be moved horizontally and vertically using the arrow keys.

To prevent this item from moving outside of the screen, we will limit its movements inside the canvas dimensions:

```python
import tkinter as tk

class App(tk.Tk):
    def __init__(self):
        super().__init__()
        self.title("Moving canvas items")

        self.canvas = tk.Canvas(self, bg="white")
        self.canvas.pack()
        self.update()
        self.width = self.canvas.winfo_width()
        self.height = self.canvas.winfo_height()

        self.item = self.canvas.create_rectangle(30, 30, 60, 60,
                                                  fill="blue")
        self.pressed_keys = {}
        self.bind("<KeyPress>", self.key_press)
        self.bind("<KeyRelease>", self.key_release)
        self.process_movements()

    def key_press(self, event):
        self.pressed_keys[event.keysym] = True

    def key_release(self, event):
        self.pressed_keys.pop(event.keysym, None)

    def process_movements(self):
        off_x, off_y = 0, 0
        speed = 3
        if 'Right' in self.pressed_keys:
            off_x += speed
        if 'Left' in self.pressed_keys:
            off_x -= speed
        if 'Down' in self.pressed_keys:
            off_y += speed
        if 'Up' in self.pressed_keys:
            off_y -= speed

        x0, y0, x1, y1 = self.canvas.coords(self.item)
```

```
                pos_x = x0 + (x1 - x0) / 2 + off_x
                pos_y = y0 + (y1 - y0) / 2 + off_y
                if 0 <= pos_x <= self.width and 0 <= pos_y <= self.height:
                    self.canvas.move(self.item, off_x, off_y)

                self.after(10, self.process_movements)

    if __name__ == "__main__":
        app = App()
        app.mainloop()
```

How it works...

To handle the arrow keyboard events, we bind the `"<KeyPress>"` and `"<KeyRelease>"` sequences to the application instance. The currently pressed key symbols are stored in the `pressed_keys` dictionary:

```
    def __init__(self):
        # ...
        self.pressed_keys = {}
        self.bind("<KeyPress>", self.key_press)
        self.bind("<KeyRelease>", self.key_release)

    def key_press(self, event):
        self.pressed_keys[event.keysym] = True

    def key_release(self, event):
        self.pressed_keys.pop(event.keysym, None)
```

This approach is preferred instead of separately binding the `"<Up>"`, `"<Down>"`, `"<Right>"`, and `"<Left>"` keys, because that would call each handler only when Tkinter processes the input keyboard events, causing the item to "jump" from one position to the next one rather than moving it smoothly on the horizontal and vertical axes.

The last sentence of the initialization of the `App` instance is the call to `process_movements()`, which starts processing the movement of the canvas item.

This method calculates the offset in each axis that the item should be displaced. Depending on the contents of the `pressed_keys` dictionary, the `speed` value is added or subtracted on each component of the coordinates:

```
    def process_movements(self):
        off_x, off_y = 0, 0
        speed = 3
```

```
if 'Right' in self.pressed_keys:
    off_x += speed
if 'Left' in self.pressed_keys:
    off_x -= speed
if 'Down' in self.pressed_keys:
    off_y += speed
if 'Up' in self.pressed_keys:
    off_y -= speed
```

After this, we retrieve the current item position by calling `canvas.coords()` and unpacking the couple of points that form the bounding box into four variables.

The center of the item is calculated by adding the x and y components of the upper-left corner to half of its width and height. This result, plus the offset in each axis, corresponds to the final position of the item after it is moved:

```
x0, y0, x1, y1 = self.canvas.coords(self.item)
pos_x = x0 + (x1 - x0) / 2 + off_x
pos_y = y0 + (y1 - y0) / 2 + off_y
```

Then, we check whether this final item position is within the canvas area. To do so, we take advantage of Python's support for chaining comparison operators:

```
if 0 <= pos_x <= self.width and 0 <= pos_y <= self.height:
    self.canvas.move(self.item, off_x, off_y)
```

Finally, this method schedules itself with a delay of 10 milliseconds by calling `self.after(10, self.process_movements)`. Thus, we achieve the effect of having a "custom mainloop" inside Tkinter's mainloop.

There's more...

You might wonder why we did not call `after_idle()` instead of `after()` to schedule the `process_movements()` method.

It might look a valid approach since there are no other events to process, apart from redrawing our canvas and handling keyboard inputs, so there is no need to add a delay between calls to `process_movements()` if there are no pending GUI events.

However, using `after_idle` would cause the item to move at a pace that will depend on the computer speed. This means that a fast system will call `process_movements()` more times in the same interval of time than a slower one, and this difference will be noticeable in the item speed.

By introducing a minimum fixed delay, we give a chance to machines with different capabilities to behave in a similar manner.

See also

- The *Detecting collisions between items* recipe

Detecting collisions between items

As a continuation of the preceding recipe, we can detect whether a rectangle item overlaps with another one. In fact, this can be achieved, assuming that we are working with shapes contained in rectangular boxes, using the `find_overlapping()` method from the `Canvas` class.

Getting ready

This application extends the preceding one by adding four green rectangles to the canvas and highlighting the one that is touched by a blue rectangle moved using the arrow keys:

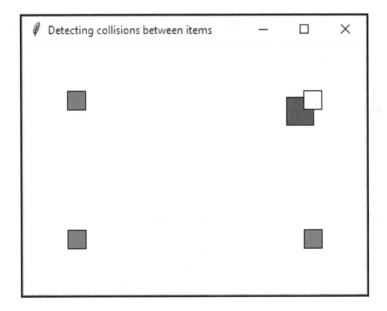

How to do it...

Since this script has many similarities with the preceding one, we marked the parts of the code that create the four rectangles and invoke the `canvas.find_overlapping()` method:

```python
import tkinter as tk

class App(tk.Tk):
    def __init__(self):
        super().__init__()
        self.title("Detecting collisions between items")

        self.canvas = tk.Canvas(self, bg="white")
        self.canvas.pack()
        self.update()
        self.width = w = self.canvas.winfo_width()
        self.height = h = self.canvas.winfo_height()

        pos = (w/2 - 15, h/2 - 15, w/2 + 15, h/2 + 15)
        self.item = self.canvas.create_rectangle(*pos, fill="blue")
        positions = [(60, 60), (w-60, 60), (60, h-60), (w-60, h-60)]
        for x, y in positions:
            self.canvas.create_rectangle(x-10, y-10, x+10, y+10,
                                         fill="green")
        self.pressed_keys = {}
        self.bind("<KeyPress>", self.key_press)
        self.bind("<KeyRelease>", self.key_release)
        self.process_movements()

    def key_press(self, event):
        self.pressed_keys[event.keysym] = True

    def key_release(self, event):
        self.pressed_keys.pop(event.keysym, None)

    def process_movements(self):
        all_items = self.canvas.find_all()
        for item in filter(lambda i: i is not self.item, all_items):
            self.canvas.itemconfig(item, fill="green")

        x0, y0, x1, y1 = self.canvas.coords(self.item)
        items = self.canvas.find_overlapping(x0, y0, x1, y1)
        for item in filter(lambda i: i is not self.item, items):
            self.canvas.itemconfig(item, fill="yellow")

        off_x, off_y = 0, 0
        speed = 3
```

```
        if 'Right' in self.pressed_keys:
            off_x += speed
        if 'Left' in self.pressed_keys:
            off_x -= speed
        if 'Down' in self.pressed_keys:
            off_y += speed
        if 'Up' in self.pressed_keys:
            off_y -= speed

        pos_x = x0 + (x1 - x0) / 2 + off_x
        pos_y = y0 + (y1 - y0) / 2 + off_y
        if 0 <= pos_x <= self.width and 0 <= pos_y <= self.height:
            self.canvas.move(self.item, off_x, off_y)

        self.after(10, self.process_movements)

if __name__ == "__main__":
    app = App()
    app.mainloop()
```

How it works...

The modification to the __init__ method is similar to the one in the *Finding items by their position* recipe, so you can review it in case you have any doubts and skip directly to the changes in the process_movements() method.

Before we calculate any overlap, the fill color of all the canvas items, except the one that can be controlled by the user, is changed to green. These item's identifiers are retrieved by the canvas.find_all() method:

```
def process_movements(self):
    all_items = self.canvas.find_all()
    for item in filter(lambda i: i != self.item, all_items):
        self.canvas.itemconfig(item, fill="green")
```

Now that the item colors are reset, we call `canvas.find_overlapping()` to get all the items that are currently colliding with the moving item. Again, the item controlled by the user is excluded from the loop, and the color of the rest of the overlapping items (if any) is changed to yellow:

```
def process_movements(self):
    # ...

    x0, y0, x1, y1 = self.canvas.coords(self.item)
    items = self.canvas.find_overlapping(x0, y0, x1, y1)
    for item in filter(lambda i: i != self.item, items):
        self.canvas.itemconfig(item, fill="yellow")
```

The method continues its execution by moving the blue rectangle by the calculated offset, and scheduling `process_movements()` itself again.

There's more...

If you want to detect when the moving item fully overlaps another one, instead of partially doing it, replace the call to `canvas.find_overlapping()` to `canvas.find_enclosed()` with the same parameters.

Deleting items from a canvas

Besides adding and modifying items on a canvas, it is also possible to delete them via the `delete()` method of the `Canvas` class. Although the usage of this method is very straightforward, there are a couple of useful patterns that we will see in the next example.

Keep in mind that the more items displayed on a canvas, the longer it will take to Tkinter to redraw the widget. Therefore, it is convenient to remove unnecessary items if this could cause a performance issue.

Getting ready

For this recipe, we will build an application that randomly displays several circles on a canvas. Each circle removes itself once you click on it, and the window contains one button to clear all the items and another button to start over again:

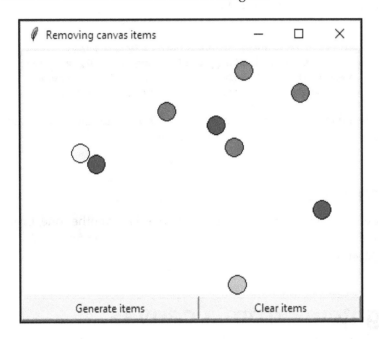

How to do it...

To irregularly place the items on the canvas, we will generate the coordinates using the `randint` function from the `random` module. The item color will be randomly chosen as well by calling `choice` with a predefined list of colors.

Once generated, items can be deleted either by triggering the `on_click` handler when clicked or by pressing the Clear items button, which executes the `clear_all` callback. These methods internally call `canvas.delete()` with the appropriate parameters:

```
import random
import tkinter as tk

class App(tk.Tk):
    colors = ("red", "yellow", "green", "blue", "orange")
```

```python
    def __init__(self):
        super().__init__()
        self.title("Removing canvas items")

        self.canvas = tk.Canvas(self, bg="white")
        frame = tk.Frame(self)
        generate_btn = tk.Button(frame, text="Generate items",
                                    command=self.generate_items)
        clear_btn = tk.Button(frame, text="Clear items",
                                command=self.clear_items)

        self.canvas.pack()
        frame.pack(fill=tk.BOTH)
        generate_btn.pack(side=tk.LEFT, expand=True, fill=tk.BOTH)
        clear_btn.pack(side=tk.LEFT, expand=True, fill=tk.BOTH)

        self.update()
        self.width = self.canvas.winfo_width()
        self.height = self.canvas.winfo_height()

        self.canvas.bind("<Button-1>", self.on_click)
        self.generate_items()

    def on_click(self, event):
        item = self.canvas.find_withtag(tk.CURRENT)
        self.canvas.delete(item)

    def generate_items(self):
        self.clear_items()
        for _ in range(10):
            x = random.randint(0, self.width)
            y = random.randint(0, self.height)
            color = random.choice(self.colors)
            self.canvas.create_oval(x, y, x + 20, y + 20, fill=color)

    def clear_items(self):
        self.canvas.delete(tk.ALL)

if __name__ == "__main__":
    app = App()
    app.mainloop()
```

How it works...

The `canvas.delete()` method takes one argument, which can be an item identifier or a tag, and removes the matching item or items, since the same tag can be used multiple times.

In the `on_click()` handler, we can see an example of how to remove an item by its identifier:

```
def on_click(self, event):
    item = self.canvas.find_withtag(tk.CURRENT)
    self.canvas.delete(item)
```

Note that if we click on an empty point, `canvas.find_withtag(tk.CURRENT)` will return `None`, but it will not raise any error when passed to `canvas.delete()`. This happens because the `None` parameter will not match any item identifier or tag and therefore, it is a valid value even though it will not perform any action.

In the `clear_items()` callback, we can find another example of deleting items. Here, instead of passing an item identifier, we used the `ALL` tag to match all the items and remove them from the canvas:

```
def clear_items(self):
    self.canvas.delete(tk.ALL)
```

As you may have noticed, the `ALL` tag works out of the box and does not need to be added to every canvas item.

Binding events to canvas items

So far, we have seen how to bind events to widgets; however, it is also possible to do so for canvas items. This helps us to write more specific and simpler event handlers, instead of binding all the types of events we want to process on the `Canvas` instance and then determining which action has to be applied according to the affected item.

Getting ready

The following application shows how to implement the drag and drop functionality on canvas items. This is a common functionality that serves to illustrate how this approach can simplify our programs.

How to do it...

We will create a couple of items that can be dragged and dropped with the mouse—a rectangle and an oval. The different shapes help us to note how the click events are correctly applied to the corresponding item, even though the items are placed overlapping each other:

```python
import tkinter as tk

class App(tk.Tk):
    def __init__(self):
        super().__init__()
        self.title("Drag and drop")

        self.dnd_item = None
        self.canvas = tk.Canvas(self, bg="white")
        self.canvas.pack()

        self.canvas.create_rectangle(30, 30, 60, 60, fill="green",
                                     tags="draggable")
        self.canvas.create_oval(120, 120, 150, 150, fill="red",
                                tags="draggable")
        self.canvas.tag_bind("draggable", "<ButtonPress-1>",
                             self.button_press)
        self.canvas.tag_bind("draggable", "<Button1-Motion>",
                             self.button_motion)

    def button_press(self, event):
        item = self.canvas.find_withtag(tk.CURRENT)
        self.dnd_item = (item, event.x, event.y)

    def button_motion(self, event):
        x, y = event.x, event.y
        item, x0, y0 = self.dnd_item
        self.canvas.move(item, x - x0, y - y0)
        self.dnd_item = (item, x, y)

if __name__ == "__main__":
    app = App()
    app.mainloop()
```

How it works...

To bind events to items, we use the `tag_bind()` method from the `Canvas` class. This adds the event binding to all the items that match the item specifier, in our example, the `"draggable"` tag.

Even the method is named `tag_bind()`; it would be also valid to pass an item identifier instead of a tag:

```
self.canvas.tag_bind("draggable", "<ButtonPress-1>",
                        self.button_press)
self.canvas.tag_bind("draggable", "<Button1-Motion>",
                        self.button_motion)
```

Keep in mind that this only affects existing tagged items, so if we add new items later on with the `"draggable"` tag, they will not have these bindings attached.

The `button_press()` method is the handler invoked when an item is clicked. As usual, a common pattern to retrieve the clicked item is to call `canvas.find_withtag(tk.CURRENT)`.

This item identifier and the x and y coordinates of the `click` event are stored in the `dnd_item` field. These values will be used later to move the item in sync with the mouse motion:

```
def button_press(self, event):
    item = self.canvas.find_withtag(tk.CURRENT)
    self.dnd_item = (item, event.x, event.y)
```

The `button_motion()` method processes the mouse motion events while the primary button is being held.

To set the distance that the item should be moved, we calculate the difference from the current event position to the previously stored coordinates. These values are passed to the `canvas.move()` method and saved again in the `dnd_item` field:

```
def button_motion(self, event):
    x, y = event.x, event.y
    item, x0, y0 = self.dnd_item
    self.canvas.move(item, x - x0, y - y0)
    self.dnd_item = (item, x, y)
```

There are some variations of this drag and drop functionality that also implement a handler for the `<ButtonRelease-1>` sequence, which unsets the currently dragged item.

However, this is not necessary because once this type of event occurs, the `<Button1-Motion>` binding will not be triggered until an item is clicked again. This also saves us from checking whether `dnd_item` is not `None` at the beginning of the `button_motion()` handler.

There's more...

It is possible to improve this example by adding some basic validations, such as verifying that users cannot drop an item outside of the canvas visible area.

To implement this, you can use the patterns we have covered in previous recipes to calculate the canvas width and height and verify that the final position of the item is inside a valid range by chaining the comparison operators. You can use the structure shown in the following snippet as a template:

```
final_x, final_y = pos_x + off_x, pos_y + off_y
if 0 <= final_x <= canvas_width and 0 <= final_y <= canvas_height:
    canvas.move(item, off_x, off_y)
```

See also

- The *Moving canvas items* recipe

Rendering a canvas into a PostScript file

The `Canvas` class natively supports saving its contents using the PostScript language via its `postscript()` method. This stores the graphical representation of canvas items, such as lines, rectangles, polygons, ovals, and arcs, however, it does not do so for embedded widgets and images.

We will modify a previous recipe that dynamically generates this type of simple items to add the functionality to save a representation of the canvas into a PostScript file.

How to do it...

We will take the code sample from the *Drawing lines and arrows* recipe to add a button to print the canvas contents to a PostScript file:

```
import tkinter as tk

class App(tk.Tk):
    def __init__(self):
        super().__init__()
        self.title("Basic canvas")

        self.line_start = None
        self.form = LineForm(self)
        self.render_btn = tk.Button(self, text="Render canvas",
                                    command=self.render_canvas)
        self.canvas = tk.Canvas(self, bg="white")
        self.canvas.bind("<Button-1>", self.draw)

        self.form.grid(row=0, column=0, padx=10, pady=10)
        self.render_btn.grid(row=1, column=0)
        self.canvas.grid(row=0, column=1, rowspan=2)

    def draw(self, event):
        # ...

    def render_canvas(self):
        self.canvas.postscript(file="output.ps", colormode="color")
```

How it works...

The main addition to the original script is the `Render canvas` button with the `render_canvas()` callback.

It calls the `postscript()` method on the `canvas` instance with the `file` and `colormode` arguments. These options specify the path to the destination file that writes the PostScript and the output color information, which could be `"color"` for full color output, `"gray"` to translate to gray-scale equivalents, and `"mono"` to convert all colors to black or white:

```
    def render_canvas(self):
        self.canvas.postscript(file="output.ps", colormode="color")
```

You can check all the valid options that can be passed to the `postscript()` method on the Tk/Tcl documentation at `https://www.tcl.tk/man/tcl8.6/TkCmd/canvas.htm#M61`. Bear in mind that PostScript is a language primarily aimed to be printed, so most options refer to page settings.

There's more...

Since PostScript files are not as popular as other file formats, you might want to convert the generated file from PostScript to a more familiar format such as PDF.

To do so, you need a third-party software, such as **Ghostscript**, which is distributed under GNU's **Affero General Public License** (**AGPL**). Ghostscript's interpreter and renderer utilities can be invoked from your program to automatically convert the PostScript result to PDF.

Download and install the latest version of the software from `https://www.ghostscript.com/download/gsdnld.html` and add the `bin` and `lib` folders of the installation into your operating system path.

Then, modify your Tkinter application to call the `ps2pdf` program as a subprocess and remove the `output.ps` file when it finish its execution, as follows:

```python
import os
import subprocess
import tkinter as tk

class App(tk.Tk):
    # ...

    def render_canvas(self):
        output_filename = "output.ps"
        self.canvas.postscript(file=output_filename, colormode="color")
        process = subprocess.run(["ps2pdf", output_filename, "output.pdf"],
                                 shell=True)
        os.remove(output_filename)
```

8
Themed Widgets

In this chapter, we will cover the following recipes:

- Replacing basic widget classes
- Creating an editable drop-down with Combobox
- Using the Treeview widget
- Populating nested items in a Treeview
- Displaying tabbable panes with Notebook
- Applying Ttk styling
- Creating a datepicker widget

Introduction

Tk-themed widgets are a separate collection of Tk widgets, which have a native look and feel, and their style can be highly customized using a specific API.

These classes are defined in the `tkinter.ttk` module. Apart from defining new widgets such as Treeview and Notebook, this module redefines the implementation of classic Tk widgets such as Button, Label, and Frame.

In this chapter, we will cover not only how to change our application Tk widgets for themed widgets, but also how to style them and use the new widget classes.

The themed Tk widget set was introduced in Tk 8.5, which should not be a problem since Python 3.6 installers let you include version 8.6 of the Tcl/Tk interpreter.

However, you can verify it on any platform by running `python -m tkinter` from the command line, which starts the following program that outputs the Tcl/Tk version:

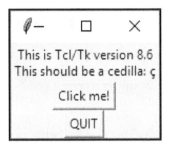

Replacing basic widget classes

As a first approach to themed Tkinter classes, we will take a look at how to use the same widgets (Buttons, Labels, Entries, and so on) from this different module, keeping the same behavior in our application.

Although this will not give us the full potential of their styling capabilities, we can easily appreciate the visual variations that bring the native look and feel of themed widgets.

Getting ready

In the following screenshot, you can note the differences between a GUI with themed widgets and the same window using standard Tkinter widgets:

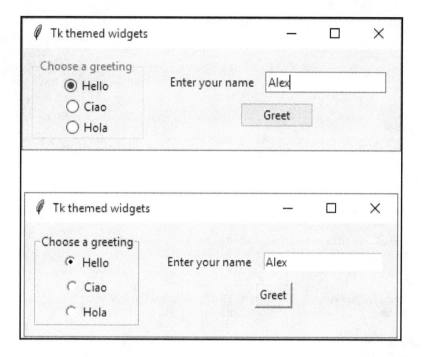

We will build the application shown in the first window, but we will also learn how to easily switch between both styles.

Note that this is highly platform dependent. In this case, the themed variation corresponds to how themed widgets look on Windows 10.

How to do it...

To start using themed widgets, all you need is to import the `tkinter.ttk` module and use the widgets defined there in your Tkinter application as usual:

```
import tkinter as tk
import tkinter.ttk as ttk

class App(tk.Tk):
    greetings = ("Hello", "Ciao", "Hola")

    def __init__(self):
        super().__init__()
        self.title("Tk themed widgets")

        var = tk.StringVar()
```

```
        var.set(self.greetings[0])
        label_frame = ttk.LabelFrame(self, text="Choose a greeting")
        for greeting in self.greetings:
            radio = ttk.Radiobutton(label_frame, text=greeting,
                                    variable=var, value=greeting)
            radio.pack()

        frame = ttk.Frame(self)
        label = ttk.Label(frame, text="Enter your name")
        entry = ttk.Entry(frame)

        command = lambda: print("{}, {}!".format(var.get(),
                                        entry.get()))
        button = ttk.Button(frame, text="Greet", command=command)

        label.grid(row=0, column=0, padx=5, pady=5)
        entry.grid(row=0, column=1, padx=5, pady=5)
        button.grid(row=1, column=0, columnspan=2, pady=5)

        label_frame.pack(side=tk.LEFT, padx=10, pady=10)
        frame.pack(side=tk.LEFT, padx=10, pady=10)

if __name__ == "__main__":
    app = App()
    app.mainloop()
```

In case you want to run the same program with regular Tkinter widgets, replace all `ttk.` occurrences with `tk.`.

How it works...

A common way to start using themed widgets is to import the `tkinter.ttk` module using the `import ... as` syntax. Thus, we can easily identify standard widgets with the `tk` name and themed widget with the `ttk` name:

```
import tkinter as tk
import tkinter.ttk as ttk
```

As you might have noticed in the preceding code, replacing widgets from the `tkinter` module with their equivalents from `tkinter.ttk` is as easy as changing the alias name:

```
import tkinter as tk
import tkinter.ttk as ttk

# ...
```

```
entry_1 = tk.Entry(root)
entry_2 = ttk.Entry(root)
```

In our example, we did so for the ttk.Frame, ttk.Label, ttk.Entry, ttk.LabelFrame, and ttk.Radiobutton widgets. These classes accept almost the same basic options as their standard Tkinter equivalents; indeed, they actually are their subclasses.

However, this translation is simple because we are not porting any styling options, such as foreground or background. In themed widgets, these keywords are used separately through the ttk.Style class, which we will cover in another recipe.

See also

- The *Applying Ttk styling* recipe

Creating an editable drop-down with Combobox

Drop-down lists are a succinct way of choosing a value by vertically displaying a list of values only when needed. This is also common to let users input another option that is not present in the list.

This functionality is combined in the ttk.Combobox class, which takes the native look and feel of your platform drop-downs.

Getting ready

Our next application will consist of a simple drop-down entry with a couple of buttons to confirm the selection or clear its contents.

If one of the predefined values is selected or the **Submit** button is clicked, the current Combobox value is printed in the standard output, as follows:

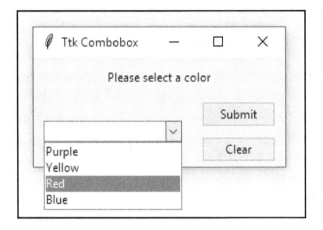

How to do it...

Our application creates a ttk.Combobox instance during its initialization, passing a predefined sequence of values that can be selected in the drop-down list:

```
import tkinter as tk
import tkinter.ttk as ttk

class App(tk.Tk):
    def __init__(self):
        super().__init__()
        self.title("Ttk Combobox")
        colors = ("Purple", "Yellow", "Red", "Blue")

        self.label = ttk.Label(self, text="Please select a color")
        self.combo = ttk.Combobox(self, values=colors)
        btn_submit = ttk.Button(self, text="Submit",
                                command=self.display_color)
        btn_clear = ttk.Button(self, text="Clear",
                               command=self.clear_color)

        self.combo.bind("<<ComboboxSelected>>", self.display_color)

        self.label.pack(pady=10)
        self.combo.pack(side=tk.LEFT, padx=10, pady=5)
        btn_submit.pack(side=tk.TOP, padx=10, pady=5)
```

```
        btn_clear.pack(padx=10, pady=5)

    def display_color(self, *args):
        color = self.combo.get()
        print("Your selection is", color)

    def clear_color(self):
        self.combo.set("")

if __name__ == "__main__":
    app = App()
    app.mainloop()
```

How it works...

As usual, the `ttk.Combobox` widget is added to our application by passing the `Tk` instance as the first parameter to its constructor. The `values` option specifies the list of selectable choices that are displayed when the drop-down arrow is clicked.

We bind the `"<<ComboboxSelected>>"` virtual event that is generated when one of the choices from the list of values is selected:

```
        self.label = ttk.Label(self, text="Please select a color")
        self.combo = ttk.Combobox(self, values=colors)
        btn_submit = ttk.Button(self, text="Submit",
                                command=self.display_color)
        btn_clear = ttk.Button(self, text="Clear",
                               command=self.clear_color)

        self.combo.bind("<<ComboboxSelected>>", self.display_color)
```

The same method is invoked when you click on the `Submit` button, so it receives a value input by the user.

We defined that `display_color()` takes a variable list of arguments using the `*` syntax to safely handle optional arguments. This happens because an event is passed to it when invoked through event binding, but it does not receive any parameters when invoked from the button callback.

Within this method, we retrieve the current Combobox value via its `get()` method and print it in the standard output:

```
def display_color(self, *args):
    color = self.combo.get()
    print("Your selection is", color)
```

Finally, `clear_color()` clears the contents of the Combobox by calling its `set()` method with the empty string:

```
def clear_color(self):
    self.combo.set("")
```

With these methods, we have explored how to interact with the current selection of a Combobox instance.

There's more...

The `ttk.Combobox` class extends `ttk.Entry`, which in turn extends the `Entry` class from the `tkinter` module.

This means that we could also use the methods that we have already covered from the `Entry` class if needed:

```
combobox.insert(0, "Add this at the beginning: ")
```

The preceding code is more straightforward than `combobox.set("Add this at the beginning: " + combobox.get())`.

Using the Treeview widget

In this recipe, we will introduce the `ttk.Treeview` class, a versatile widget that lets us display information in both tabular and hierarchical structures.

Each item added to the `ttk.Treeview` class is divided into one or more columns, where the first one may contain text and an icon and serves to indicate whether the item can be expanded and show more nested items. The rest of the columns contain the values that we want to display for each row.

The first row of the `ttk.Treeview` class is composed of headings that identify each column by its name and can be optionally hidden.

Getting ready

Using `ttk.Treeview`, we will tabulate the information of a list of contacts stored in a CSV file, similar to what we previously did in `Chapter 5`, *Object-Oriented Programming and MVC*:

Last name	First name	Email
Gauford	Albertine	agauford0@acme.com
Greger	Bryce	bgreger1@acme.com
Wetherald	Rickey	rwetherald2@acme.com
Onthank	Giustina	gonthank3@acme.com
Clever	Ulric	uclever4@acme.com
Guthrum	Amble	aguthrum5@acme.com
Guppey	Austine	aguppey6@acme.com
Farndale	Gerhardt	gfarndale7@acme.com
Wolfenden	Caressa	cwolfenden8@acme.com
Holliar	Robbyn	rholliar9@acme.com

Ttk Treeview

How to do it...

We will create a `ttk.Treeview` widget with three columns that hold the fields of each contact: one for its last name, another one for its first name, and the last one for its email address.

Contacts are loaded from a CSV file using the `csv` module, and then we add the binding for the `"<<TreeviewSelect>>"` virtual element, which is generated when one or more items are selected:

```
import csv
import tkinter as tk
import tkinter.ttk as ttk

class App(tk.Tk):
    def __init__(self, path):
        super().__init__()
```

```
        self.title("Ttk Treeview")

        columns = ("#1", "#2", "#3")
        self.tree = ttk.Treeview(self, show="headings", columns=columns)
        self.tree.heading("#1", text="Last name")
        self.tree.heading("#2", text="First name")
        self.tree.heading("#3", text="Email")
        ysb = ttk.Scrollbar(self, orient=tk.VERTICAL,
                            command=self.tree.yview)
        self.tree.configure(yscroll=ysb.set)

        with open("contacts.csv", newline="") as f:
            for contact in csv.reader(f):
                self.tree.insert("", tk.END, values=contact)
        self.tree.bind("<<TreeviewSelect>>", self.print_selection)

        self.tree.grid(row=0, column=0)
        ysb.grid(row=0, column=1, sticky=tk.N + tk.S)
        self.rowconfigure(0, weight=1)
        self.columnconfigure(0, weight=1)

    def print_selection(self, event):
        for selection in self.tree.selection():
            item = self.tree.item(selection)
            last_name, first_name, email = item["values"][0:3]
            text = "Selection: {}, {} <{}>"
            print(text.format(last_name, first_name, email))

if __name__ == "__main__":
    app = App()
    app.mainloop()
```

If you run this program, each time you select a contact, its details will be printed in the
standard output as a way to illustrate how to retrieve the data of a selected row.

How it works...

To create a ttk.Treeview with multiple columns, we need to indicate the identifiers of
each one with the columns option. Then, we can configure the header text by calling the
heading() method.

We used identifiers #1, #2, and #3 since the first column, which contains the expandable
icon and text, is always generated with the #0 identifier.

Also we passed the `"headings"` value to the `show` option to indicate that we want to hide the `#0` column, because there will not be nested items.

The following values are valid for the `show` option:

- `"tree"`: Displays column `#0`
- `"headings"`: Displays the header row
- `"tree headings"`: Displays both column `#0` and the header row—this is the default value
- `""`: Does not display column `#0` or the header row

After this, we attached a vertical scroll bar to our `ttk.Treeview` widget:

```
columns = ("#1", "#2", "#3")
self.tree = ttk.Treeview(self, show="headings", columns=columns)
self.tree.heading("#1", text="Last name")
self.tree.heading("#2", text="First name")
self.tree.heading("#3", text="Email")
ysb = ttk.Scrollbar(self, orient=tk.VERTICAL,
command=self.tree.yview)
self.tree.configure(yscroll=ysb.set)
```

To load the contacts into the table, we process the file with the `reader()` function from the `csv` module, and the row read in each iteration is added to `ttk.Treeview`.

This is done by calling the `insert()` method, which receives the parent node and the position to place the item.

Since all contacts are shown as top-level items, we pass an empty string as the first parameter and the `END` constant to indicate that each new item is inserted at the last position.

You can optionally provide some keyword arguments to the `insert()` method. Here, we specified the `values` option, which takes the sequence of values that is displayed in each column of the Treeview:

```
with open("contacts.csv", newline="") as f:
    for contact in csv.reader(f):
        self.tree.insert("", tk.END, values=contact)
self.tree.bind("<<TreeviewSelect>>", self.print_selection)
```

The <<TreeviewSelect>> event is the virtual event generated when the user selects one or more items from the table. Within the print_selection() handler, we retrieve the current selection by calling the selection() method, and for each result, we will perform the following steps:

1. With the item() method, we get the dictionary of options and values of the selected item
2. We retrieve the first three values from the item dictionary, which correspond to the last name, first name, and email of the contact
3. The values are formatted and printed into the standard output:

```
def print_selection(self, event):
    for selection in self.tree.selection():
        item = self.tree.item(selection)
        last_name, first_name, email = item["values"][0:3]
        text = "Selection: {}, {} <{}>"
        print(text.format(last_name, first_name, email))
```

There's more...

So far, we have covered some basic aspects of the ttk.Treeview class since we are using it as a regular table. However, it is also possible to extend our existing application with more advanced features.

Using tags in Treeview items

Tags are available for ttk.Treeview items, so it is possible to bind event sequences for specific rows of our contacts table.

Let's suppose that we want to open a new window to write an email to a contact when we double-click on it; however, this should only work for records where the email field is filled in.

We can easily implement this by conditionally adding a tag to the items while inserting them, and then calling `tag_bind()` on the widget instance with the `"<Double-Button-1>"` sequence—here we simply refer to the implementation of the `send_email_to_contact()` handler function by its name:

```
columns = ("Last name", "First name", "Email")
tree = ttk.Treeview(self, show="headings", columns=columns)

for contact in csv.reader(f):
    email = contact[2]
    tags = ("dbl-click",) if email else ()
    self.tree.insert("", tk.END, values=contact, tags=tags)

tree.tag_bind("dbl-click", "<Double-Button-1>", send_email_to_contact)
```

Similar to what happens when binding events to `Canvas` items, always remember to add the tagged items to `ttk.Treeview` before calling `tag_bind()`, because the bindings are only added to existing matching items.

See also

- The *Populating nested items in a Treeview* recipe

Populating nested items in a Treeview

While `ttk.Treeview` can be used as a regular table, it may also contain hierarchical structures. This is shown as a tree where items can be expanded to see more nodes of the hierarchy.

This is useful to display the results of recursive calls and several levels of nested items. In this recipe, we will take a look at a common scenario that fits with this kind of structure.

Getting ready

To illustrate how to recursively add items in a `ttk.Treeview` widget, we will create a basic filesystem browser. Expandable nodes will represent folders, and once opened, they will show the files and folders that they contain:

How to do it...

The tree will be initially populated by the `populate_node()` method, which lists the entries in the current directory. If an entry is a directory, it also adds an empty child to show it as an expandable node.

When a node that represents a directory is opened, it lazily loads the contents of the directory by calling `populate_node()` again. This time, instead of adding the items as top-level nodes, they are nested inside the opened node:

```python
import os
import tkinter as tk
import tkinter.ttk as ttk

class App(tk.Tk):
    def __init__(self, path):
        super().__init__()
```

```
            self.title("Ttk Treeview")

            abspath = os.path.abspath(path)
            self.nodes = {}
            self.tree = ttk.Treeview(self)
            self.tree.heading("#0", text=abspath, anchor=tk.W)
            ysb = ttk.Scrollbar(self, orient=tk.VERTICAL,
                                command=self.tree.yview)
            xsb = ttk.Scrollbar(self, orient=tk.HORIZONTAL,
                                command=self.tree.xview)
            self.tree.configure(yscroll=ysb.set, xscroll=xsb.set)

            self.tree.grid(row=0, column=0, sticky=tk.N + tk.S + tk.E +
    tk.W)
            ysb.grid(row=0, column=1, sticky=tk.N + tk.S)
            xsb.grid(row=1, column=0, sticky=tk.E + tk.W)
            self.rowconfigure(0, weight=1)
            self.columnconfigure(0, weight=1)

            self.tree.bind("<<TreeviewOpen>>", self.open_node)
            self.populate_node("", abspath)

        def populate_node(self, parent, abspath):
            for entry in os.listdir(abspath):
                entry_path = os.path.join(abspath, entry)
                node = self.tree.insert(parent, tk.END, text=entry, open=False)
                if os.path.isdir(entry_path):
                    self.nodes[node] = entry_path
                    self.tree.insert(node, tk.END)

        def open_node(self, event):
            item = self.tree.focus()
            abspath = self.nodes.pop(item, False)
            if abspath:
                children = self.tree.get_children(item)
                self.tree.delete(children)
                self.populate_node(item, abspath)

if __name__ == "__main__":
    app = App(path=".")
    app.mainloop()
```

When you run the preceding example, it will display the filesystem hierarchy from the directory where the script is located, but you can explicitly set the directory you want via the `path` argument of the `App` constructor.

How it works...

In this example, we will use the os module, which is part of the Python Standard Library and provides a portable way of performing operating system calls.

The first use of the os module is the translation of the initial path of the tree to an absolute path, as well as initializing the nodes dictionary, which will store the correspondence between expandable items and the path of the directories they represent:

```python
import os
import tkinter as tk
import tkinter.ttk as ttk

class App(tk.Tk):
    def __init__(self, path):
        # ...
        abspath = os.path.abspath(path)
        self.nodes = {}
```

For instance, os.path.abspath(".") will return the absolute version of the pathname you run the script from. We prefer this approach to using relative paths, because this saves us from any confusion when working with paths in our application.

Now, we initialize the ttk.Treeview instance with a vertical and horizontal scroll bar. The text of the icon heading will be the absolute path we calculated earlier:

```python
        self.tree = ttk.Treeview(self)
        self.tree.heading("#0", text=abspath, anchor=tk.W)
        ysb = ttk.Scrollbar(self, orient=tk.VERTICAL,
                            command=self.tree.yview)
        xsb = ttk.Scrollbar(self, orient=tk.HORIZONTAL,
                            command=self.tree.xview)
        self.tree.configure(yscroll=ysb.set, xscroll=xsb.set)
```

Then, we place the widgets using the Grid geometry manager and also make the ttk.Treeview instance automatically resizable both horizontally and vertically.

After this, we bind the "<<TreeviewOpen>>" virtual event, which is generated when an expandable item is opened to the open_node() handler and call populate_node() to load the entries of the specified directory:

```python
        self.tree.bind("<<TreeviewOpen>>", self.open_node)
        self.populate_node("", abspath)
```

Note that the first call to this method is made with the empty string as the parent directory, which means that they do not have any parent and are displayed as top-level items.

Within the `populate_node()` method, we list the names of the directory entries by invoking `os.listdir()`. For each entry name, we perform the following actions:

- We calculate the absolute path of the entry. On UNIX-like systems, this is achieved by concatenating the strings with a slash, but Windows uses backslashes instead. Thanks to the `os.path.join()` method, we can safely join the paths without worrying about platform-dependent details.
- We insert the `entry` string as the last child of the indicated `parent` node. We always set that nodes to be initially closed, because we want to lazy load the nested items only when needed.
- If the entry absolute path is a directory, we add the correspondence between the node and the path in the `nodes` attribute and insert an empty child that allows the item to be expanded:

```
def populate_node(self, parent, abspath):
    for entry in os.listdir(abspath):
        entry_path = os.path.join(abspath, entry)
        node = self.tree.insert(parent, tk.END, text=entry, open=False)
        if os.path.isdir(entry_path):
            self.nodes[node] = entry_path
            self.tree.insert(node, tk.END)
```

When an expandable item is clicked, the `open_node()` handler retrieves the selected item by calling the `focus()` method of the `ttk.Treeview` instance.

This item identifier is used to get the absolute path previously added to the `nodes` attribute. To avoid raising `KeyError` if the node does not exist within the dictionary, we used its `pop()` method, which returns the second parameter as a default value—in our case, `False`.

If the node exists, we clear the "fake" item of the expandable node. Calling `self.tree.get_children(item)` returns the identifiers of the children for `item`, and then they are deleted by invoking `self.tree.delete(children)`.

Once the item is cleared, we add the "real" children entries by calling `populate_node()` with `item` as their parent:

```
def open_node(self, event):
    item = self.tree.focus()
    abspath = self.nodes.pop(item, False)
    if abspath:
        children = self.tree.get_children(item)
```

```
self.tree.delete(children)
self.populate_node(item, abspath)
```

Displaying tabbable panes with Notebook

The `ttk.Notebook` class is another of the new widget types introduced in the `ttk` module. It allows you to add many views of your application in the same window area, letting you choose the one that should be displayed by clicking on the tab associated to each view.

Tabbed panels are a good way to reuse the same portion of your GUI if the contents of multiple regions do not need to be shown at the same time.

Getting ready

The following application shows some to-do lists divided into tabs by category—lists are displayed with read-only data to simplify the example:

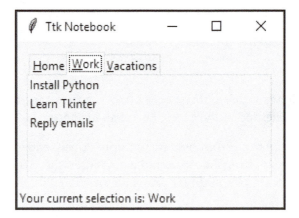

How to do it...

We instantiate the `ttk.Notebook` with a fixed size, and then loop over a dictionary with some predefined data that will serve to create the tabs and add some labels to each region:

```
import tkinter as tk
import tkinter.ttk as ttk

class App(tk.Tk):
```

```python
    def __init__(self):
        super().__init__()
        self.title("Ttk Notebook")

        todos = {
            "Home": ["Do the laundry", "Go grocery shopping"],
            "Work": ["Install Python", "Learn Tkinter", "Reply emails"],
            "Vacations": ["Relax!"]
        }

        self.notebook = ttk.Notebook(self, width=250, height=100)
        self.label = ttk.Label(self)
        for key, value in todos.items():
            frame = ttk.Frame(self.notebook)
            self.notebook.add(frame, text=key, underline=0,
                              sticky=tk.NE + tk.SW)
            for text in value:
                ttk.Label(frame, text=text).pack(anchor=tk.W)

        self.notebook.pack()
        self.label.pack(anchor=tk.W)
        self.notebook.enable_traversal()
        self.notebook.bind("<<NotebookTabChanged>>", self.select_tab)

    def select_tab(self, event):
        tab_id = self.notebook.select()
        tab_name = self.notebook.tab(tab_id, "text")
        text = "Your current selection is: {}".format(tab_name)
        self.label.config(text=text)

if __name__ == "__main__":
    app = App()
    app.mainloop()
```

Every time you click on a tab, the label at the bottom of the window updates its contents, showing the name of the current tab.

How it works...

Our `ttk.Notebook` widget is created with a specific width and height, as well as an external padding.

Each key from the `todos` dictionary is used as the name of a tab, and the list of values is added as labels to `ttk.Frame`, which represents the window region:

```
self.notebook = ttk.Notebook(self, width=250, height=100,
padding=10)
    for key, value in todos.items():
        frame = ttk.Frame(self.notebook)
        self.notebook.add(frame, text=key,
                          underline=0, sticky=tk.NE+tk.SW)
        for text in value:
            ttk.Label(frame, text=text).pack(anchor=tk.W)
```

After this, we call `enable_traversal()` on the `ttk.Notebook` widget. This allows users to switch tabs back and forth between tab panels using *Ctrl* + *Shift* + *Tab* and *Ctrl* + *Tab*, respectively.

It also enables switching into a specific tab by pressing *Alt* and the underlined character, that is, *Alt* + *H* for the `Home` tab, *Alt* + *W* for the `Work` tab, and *Alt* + *V* for the `Vacation` tab.

The `"<<NotebookTabChanged>>"` virtual event is generated when the tab selection changes, and we bind it to the `select_tab()` method. Note that this event is automatically raised when Tkinter adds a tab to `ttk.Notebook`:

```
self.notebook.pack()
self.label.pack(anchor=tk.W)
self.notebook.enable_traversal()
self.notebook.bind("<<NotebookTabChanged>>", self.select_tab)
```

When we pack the items, it is not necessary to place the `ttk.Notebook` child windows since it is internally done by the `ttk.Notebook` call to the geometry manager:

```
def select_tab(self, event):
    tab_id = self.notebook.select()
    tab_name = self.notebook.tab(tab_id, "text")
    self.label.config(text=f"Your current selection is: {tab_name}")
```

There's more...

If you want to retrieve the current displayed child of the `ttk.Notebook`, you do not need to use any extra data structures to map the tab index with the widget window.

Tkinter's `nametowidget()` method is available from all widget classes, so you can easily get the widget object that corresponds to a widget name:

```
def select_tab(self, event):
    tab_id = self.notebook.select()
    frame = self.nametowidget(tab_id)
    # Do something with the frame
```

Applying Ttk styling

As we mentioned in the first recipe of this chapter, themed widgets have a specific API to customize their appearance. We cannot directly set options, such as the foreground color or the internal padding, because these values are set via the `ttk.Style` class.

In this recipe, we will cover how to modify the widgets from the first recipe to add some styling options.

How to do it...

To add some default settings, we will simply need a `ttk.Style` object, which offers the following methods:

- `configure(style, opts)`: Changes the appearance `opts` for a widget `style`. Here is where we set options such as the foreground color, padding, and relief.
- `map(style, query)`: Changes the dynamic appearance for a widget `style`. The argument `query` is a keywords argument where each key is a styling option, and values are lists of tuples of the `(state, value)` form, meaning that the value of the option is determined by its current state.

For instance, we have marked the following examples of both situations:

```
import tkinter as tk
import tkinter.ttk as tk

class App(tk.Tk):
    def __init__(self):
        super().__init__()
        self.title("Tk themed widgets")

        style = ttk.Style(self)
        style.configure("TLabel", padding=10)
```

```
style.map("TButton",
          foreground=[("pressed", "grey"), ("active", "white")],
          background=[("pressed", "white"), ("active", "grey")]
          )
# ...
```

Now, every `ttk.Label` is displayed with a padding of `10`, and the `ttk.Button` has a dynamic styling: gray foreground and white background when the state is `pressed`, and white foreground and gray background if the state is `active`.

How it works...

Building `ttk.Style` for our applications is quite straightforward—we only need to create an instance with our parent widget as its first parameter.

Then, we can set the default styling options for our themed widgets, using an uppercase `T` plus the widget name: `TButton` for `ttk.Button`, `TLabel` for `ttk.Label`, and so on. However, there are some exceptions, so it is recommended that you check on the Python interpreter the classname by calling the `winfo_class()` method on the widget instance.

We can also add a prefix to identify a style that we do not want to use by default, but explicitly set it to some specific widgets:

```
style.configure("My.TLabel", padding=10)
# ...
label = ttk.Label(master, text="Some text", style="My.TLabel")
```

Creating a datepicker widget

If we want to let users input a date into our application, we might add a text entry that forces them to write a string with a valid date format. Another solution would be adding several numeric entries for the day, month, and year, but this would also require some validations.

Unlike other GUI frameworks, Tkinter does not include a class for this purpose; however, we can opt to apply our knowledge of themed widgets to build a Calendar widget.

Getting ready

In this recipe, we will explain a step-by-step implementation of a datepicker widget made with Ttk widgets and features:

This is a refactored version of `http://svn.python.org/projects/sandbox/trunk/ttk-gsoc/samples/ttkcalendar.py` and does not require any external packages.

How to do it...

Apart from the `tkinter` modules, we will also need the `calendar` and `datetime` modules from the Standard Library. They will help us to model and interact with the data held by the widget.

The widget header displays a couple of arrows to move the current month back and forth, based on Ttk styling options. The main body of the widget consists of a `ttk.Treeview` table, with a `Canvas` instance that highlights the selected date cell:

```python
import calendar
import datetime
import tkinter as tk
import tkinter.ttk as ttk
import tkinter.font as tkfont
from itertools import zip_longest

class TtkCalendar(ttk.Frame):
    def __init__(self, master=None, **kw):
        now = datetime.datetime.now()
```

```python
        fwday = kw.pop('firstweekday', calendar.MONDAY)
        year = kw.pop('year', now.year)
        month = kw.pop('month', now.month)
        sel_bg = kw.pop('selectbackground', '#ecffc4')
        sel_fg = kw.pop('selectforeground', '#05640e')

        super().__init__(master, **kw)

        self.selected = None
        self.date = datetime.date(year, month, 1)
        self.cal = calendar.TextCalendar(fwday)
        self.font = tkfont.Font(self)
        self.header = self.create_header()
        self.table = self.create_table()
        self.canvas = self.create_canvas(sel_bg, sel_fg)
        self.build_calendar()

    def create_header(self):
        left_arrow = {'children': [('Button.leftarrow', None)]}
        right_arrow = {'children': [('Button.rightarrow', None)]}
        style = ttk.Style(self)
        style.layout('L.TButton', [('Button.focus', left_arrow)])
        style.layout('R.TButton', [('Button.focus', right_arrow)])

        hframe = ttk.Frame(self)
        btn_left = ttk.Button(hframe, style='L.TButton',
                            command=lambda: self.move_month(-1))
        btn_right = ttk.Button(hframe, style='R.TButton',
                            command=lambda: self.move_month(1))
        label = ttk.Label(hframe, width=15, anchor='center')

        hframe.pack(pady=5, anchor=tk.CENTER)
        btn_left.grid(row=0, column=0)
        label.grid(row=0, column=1, padx=12)
        btn_right.grid(row=0, column=2)
        return label

    def move_month(self, offset):
        self.canvas.place_forget()
        month = self.date.month - 1 + offset
        year = self.date.year + month // 12
        month = month % 12 + 1
        self.date = datetime.date(year, month, 1)
        self.build_calendar()

    def create_table(self):
        cols = self.cal.formatweekheader(3).split()
        table = ttk.Treeview(self, show='', selectmode='none',
```

```
                              height=7, columns=cols)
        table.bind('<Map>', self.minsize)
        table.pack(expand=1, fill=tk.BOTH)
        table.tag_configure('header', background='grey90')
        table.insert('', tk.END, values=cols, tag='header')
        for _ in range(6):
            table.insert('', tk.END)

        width = max(map(self.font.measure, cols))
        for col in cols:
            table.column(col, width=width, minwidth=width, anchor=tk.E)
        return table

    def minsize(self, e):
        width, height = self.master.geometry().split('x')
        height = height[:height.index('+')]
        self.master.minsize(width, height)

    def create_canvas(self, bg, fg):
        canvas = tk.Canvas(self.table, background=bg,
                           borderwidth=0, highlightthickness=0)
        canvas.text = canvas.create_text(0, 0, fill=fg, anchor=tk.W)
        handler = lambda _: canvas.place_forget()
        canvas.bind('<ButtonPress-1>', handler)
        self.table.bind('<Configure>', handler)
        self.table.bind('<ButtonPress-1>', self.pressed)
        return canvas

    def build_calendar(self):
        year, month = self.date.year, self.date.month
        month_name = self.cal.formatmonthname(year, month, 0)
        month_weeks = self.cal.monthdayscalendar(year, month)

        self.header.config(text=month_name.title())
        items = self.table.get_children()[1:]
        for week, item in zip_longest(month_weeks, items):
            week = week if week else []
            fmt_week = ['%02d' % day if day else '' for day in week]
            self.table.item(item, values=fmt_week)

    def pressed(self, event):
        x, y, widget = event.x, event.y, event.widget
        item = widget.identify_row(y)
        column = widget.identify_column(x)
        items = self.table.get_children()[1:]

        if not column or not item in items:
            # clicked te header or outside the columns
```

```
            return

        index = int(column[1]) - 1
        values = widget.item(item)['values']
        text = values[index] if len(values) else None
        bbox = widget.bbox(item, column)
        if bbox and text:
            self.selected = '%02d' % text
            self.show_selection(bbox)

    def show_selection(self, bbox):
        canvas, text = self.canvas, self.selected
        x, y, width, height = bbox
        textw = self.font.measure(text)
        canvas.configure(width=width, height=height)
        canvas.coords(canvas.text, width - textw, height / 2 - 1)
        canvas.itemconfigure(canvas.text, text=text)
        canvas.place(x=x, y=y)

    @property
    def selection(self):
        if self.selected:
            year, month = self.date.year, self.date.month
            return datetime.date(year, month, int(self.selected))

def main():
    root = tk.Tk()
    root.title('Tkinter Calendar')
    ttkcal = TtkCalendar(firstweekday=calendar.SUNDAY)
    ttkcal.pack(expand=True, fill=tk.BOTH)
    root.mainloop()

if __name__ == '__main__':
    main()
```

How it works...

Our `TtkCalendar` class can be customized by passing some options as keyword arguments. They are retrieved during its initialization, with some default values in case they are not present; for example, if the current date is used for initial year and month of our calendar:

```
    def __init__(self, master=None, **kw):
        now = datetime.datetime.now()
        fwday = kw.pop('firstweekday', calendar.MONDAY)
```

```
            year = kw.pop('year', now.year)
            month = kw.pop('month', now.month)
            sel_bg = kw.pop('selectbackground', '#ecffc4')
            sel_fg = kw.pop('selectforeground', '#05640e')

            super().__init__(master, **kw)
```

Then, we define some attributes to store date information:

- `selected`: Holds the value of the selected date
- `date`: The date that represents the current month displayed on the calendar
- `calendar`: A Gregorian calendar with information on weeks and month names

The visual parts of the widget are internally instantiated in the `create_header()` and `create_table()` methods, which we will cover later.

We also used a `tkfont.Font` instance to help us to measure the font size.

Once these attributes are initialized, the visual parts of the calendar are arranged by calling the `build_calendar()` method:

```
            self.selected = None
            self.date = datetime.date(year, month, 1)
            self.cal = calendar.TextCalendar(fwday)
            self.font = tkfont.Font(self)
            self.header = self.create_header()
            self.table = self.create_table()
            self.canvas = self.create_canvas(sel_bg, sel_fg)
            self.build_calendar()
```

The `create_header()` method uses `ttk.Style` to display the arrows to move the month back and forth. It returns the label that shows the name of the current month:

```
        def create_header(self):
            left_arrow = {'children': [('Button.leftarrow', None)]}
            right_arrow = {'children': [('Button.rightarrow', None)]}
            style = ttk.Style(self)
            style.layout('L.TButton', [('Button.focus', left_arrow)])
            style.layout('R.TButton', [('Button.focus', right_arrow)])

            hframe = ttk.Frame(self)
            lbtn = ttk.Button(hframe, style='L.TButton',
                              command=lambda: self.move_month(-1))
            rbtn = ttk.Button(hframe, style='R.TButton',
                              command=lambda: self.move_month(1))
            label = ttk.Label(hframe, width=15, anchor='center')
```

```
# ...
    return label
```

The `move_month()` callback hides the current selection highlighted with the canvas field and adds the specified `offset` to the current month to set the `date` attribute with the previous or next month. Then, the calendar is redrawn again, showing the days of the new month:

```
def move_month(self, offset):
    self.canvas.place_forget()
    month = self.date.month - 1 + offset
    year = self.date.year + month // 12
    month = month % 12 + 1
    self.date = datetime.date(year, month, 1)
    self.build_calendar()
```

The calendar body is created within `create_table()` using a `ttk.Treeview` widget, which displays each week of the current month in a row:

```
def create_table(self):
    cols = self.cal.formatweekheader(3).split()
    table = ttk.Treeview(self, show='', selectmode='none',
                         height=7, columns=cols)
    table.bind('<Map>', self.minsize)
    table.pack(expand=1, fill=tk.BOTH)
    table.tag_configure('header', background='grey90')
    table.insert('', tk.END, values=cols, tag='header')
    for _ in range(6):
        table.insert('', tk.END)

    width = max(map(self.font.measure, cols))
    for col in cols:
        table.column(col, width=width, minwidth=width, anchor=tk.E)
    return table
```

The canvas that highlights the selection is instantiated within the `create_canvas()` method. Since it adjusts its size depending on the selected item dimensions, it also hides itself if the window is resized:

```
def create_canvas(self, bg, fg):
    canvas = tk.Canvas(self.table, background=bg,
                       borderwidth=0, highlightthickness=0)
    canvas.text = canvas.create_text(0, 0, fill=fg, anchor=tk.W)
    handler = lambda _: canvas.place_forget()
    canvas.bind('<ButtonPress-1>', handler)
    self.table.bind('<Configure>', handler)
    self.table.bind('<ButtonPress-1>', self.pressed)
```

```
        return canvas
```

The calendar is built by iterating over the weeks and item positions of the `ttk.Treeview` table. With the `zip_longest()` function from the `itertools` module, we iterate over the collection that contains most items and leave the missing days with an empty string:

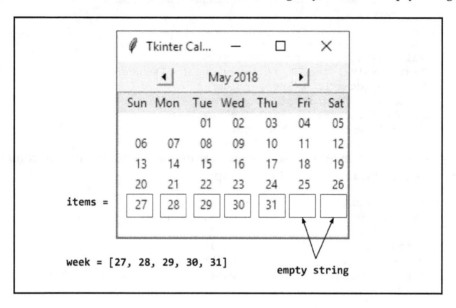

This behavior is important for the first and last week of each month, because this is where we usually find these empty spots:

```
def build_calendar(self):
    year, month = self.date.year, self.date.month
    month_name = self.cal.formatmonthname(year, month, 0)
    month_weeks = self.cal.monthdayscalendar(year, month)

    self.header.config(text=month_name.title())
    items = self.table.get_children()[1:]
    for week, item in zip_longest(month_weeks, items):
        week = week if week else []
        fmt_week = ['%02d' % day if day else '' for day in week]
        self.table.item(item, values=fmt_week)
```

When you click on a table item, the `pressed()` event handler sets the selection if the item exists, and redisplays the canvas to highlight the selection:

```
def pressed(self, event):
    x, y, widget = event.x, event.y, event.widget
```

```
item = widget.identify_row(y)
column = widget.identify_column(x)
items = self.table.get_children()[1:]

if not column or not item in items:
    # clicked te header or outside the columns
    return

index = int(column[1]) - 1
values = widget.item(item)['values']
text = values[index] if len(values) else None
bbox = widget.bbox(item, column)
if bbox and text:
    self.selected = '%02d' % text
    self.show_selection(bbox)
```

The `show_selection()` method places the canvas on the bounding box that contains the selection, measuring the text size so it fits on top of it:

```
def show_selection(self, bbox):
    canvas, text = self.canvas, self.selected
    x, y, width, height = bbox
    textw = self.font.measure(text)
    canvas.configure(width=width, height=height)
    canvas.coords(canvas.text, width - textw, height / 2 - 1)
    canvas.itemconfigure(canvas.text, text=text)
    canvas.place(x=x, y=y)
```

Finally, the `selection` property makes it possible to get the selected date as a `datetime.date` object. It is not directly used in our example, but it forms part of the API to work with the `TtkCalendar` class:

```
@property
def selection(self):
    if self.selected:
        year, month = self.date.year, self.date.month
        return datetime.date(year, month, int(self.selected))
```

See also

- The *Using the Treeview widget* recipe
- The *Applying Ttk styling* recipe

Other Books You May Enjoy

If you enjoyed this book, you may be interested in these other books by Packt:

Tkinter GUI Application Development Blueprints - Second Edition
Bhaskar Chaudhary

ISBN: 978-1-78883-746-0

- Get to know the basic concepts of GUI programming, such as Tkinter top-level widgets, geometry management, event handling, using callbacks, custom styling, and dialogs
- Create apps that can be scaled in size or complexity without breaking down the core
- Write your own GUI framework for maximum code reuse
- Build apps using both procedural and OOP styles, understanding the strengths and limitations of both styles
- Learn to structure and build large GUI applications based on Model-View-Controller (MVC) architecture
- Build multithreaded and database-driven apps
- Create apps that leverage resources from the network
- Implement mathematical concepts using Tkinter Canvas
- Develop apps that can persist application data with object serialization and tools such as configparser

Learn QT 5
Nicholas Sherriff

ISBN: 978-1-78847-885-4

- Install and configure the Qt Framework and Qt Creator IDE
- Create a new multi-project solution from scratch and control every aspect of it with QMake
- Implement a rich user interface with QML
- Learn the fundamentals of QtTest and how to integrate unit testing
- Build self-aware data entities that can serialize themselves to and from JSON
- Manage data persistence with SQLite and CRUD operations
- Reach out to the internet and consume an RSS feed
- Produce application packages for distribution to other users

Leave a review - let other readers know what you think

Please share your thoughts on this book with others by leaving a review on the site that you bought it from. If you purchased the book from Amazon, please leave us an honest review on this book's Amazon page. This is vital so that other potential readers can see and use your unbiased opinion to make purchasing decisions, we can understand what our customers think about our products, and our authors can see your feedback on the title that they have worked with Packt to create. It will only take a few minutes of your time, but is valuable to other potential customers, our authors, and Packt. Thank you!

Index

G

Ghostscript
  reference 189
GIL (Global Interpreter Lock) 137
Graphical User Interface (GUI) 8
Grid geometry manager
  using 42, 44

H

horizontal scrollbars
  creating 53, 56
HTTP requests
  performing 141, 143

I

idle tasks
  handling 151, 152
inputs
  grouping, with LabelFrame widget 50
items
  deleting, from canvas 181, 184
  finding, by position 172, 174

L

LabelFrame widget
  used, for grouping inputs 50
  used, for grouping widgets 48
lines
  drawing 160, 162
list of items
  displaying 25, 28
logical
  grouping, with LabelFrame widget 48

M

main thread 133
main window
  icon, setting 32
  size, setting 32
  title, setting 32
menu bar
  creating 92, 93
menus

variables, using 94, 96
methods
  executing, on threads 137, 140
Model-View-Controller (MVC) 109
mouse and keyboard events
  handling 28, 31
MVC pattern
  controller 126
  model 126
  used, for refactoring 125, 131
  view 126

N

Natural Language Processing (NLP) 7
nested items
  populating, in Treeview 203, 207
Notebook
  tabbable panes, displaying 208, 210
numerical values
  selecting 20, 21

O

object-oriented programming (OOP) 109
observer pattern 130
options database
  using 66, 69

P

Pack geometry manager
  using 39, 41, 42
passive model 131
Place geometry manager
  using 45, 47
PostScript file
  canvas, rendering 187
progress bar
  threads, connecting 144, 148
Python
  reference 19

R

race conditions 147
radio buttons
  used, for creating selections 22, 23